SINGER'S LIBRARY OF SONG

A VOCAL ANTHOLOGY OF MASTERWORKS AND FOLK SONGS
FROM THE MEDIEVAL ERA THROUGH THE TWENTIETH CENTURY

COMPILED AND EDITED BY PATRICK M. LIEBERGEN

D1379559

Low Book (23500)
ISBN 0-7390-3662-9
Low Book & CD (23506)
ISBN 0-7390-3664-5
Low Accompaniment CD (23503)
ISBN 0-7390-3666-1

Medium Book (23499)
ISBN 0-7390-3659-9
Medium Book & CD (23505)
ISBN 0-7390-3660-2
Medium Accompaniment CD (23502)
ISBN 0-7390-3667-X

High Book (23498)
ISBN 0-7390-3661-0
HIGH Book & CD (23504)
ISBN 0-7390-3663-7
Hi Accompaniment CD (23501)
ISBN 0-7390-3665-3

Contents

Folk Songs from the United States

Folk Songs from the British Isles

Mexico

Israel

Foreword

Singer's Library of Song features thirty-seven of the world's best-loved songs brought together for the first time in one collection. Representing a wide range of styles and composers, these songs from the medieval era through the twentieth-century are presented with historical information and suggestions for performance. Additionally, translations and pronunciation guides are included for all songs with foreign texts. Selected, edited and arranged by Patrick M. Liebergen, this truly valuable collection is an indispensable resource for the singer.

The songs are divided into two main sections. The first section of distinctive masterworks features biographies of the composers along with background information for possible use in programs. Original scores were consulted in the preparation of the editions when possible, and any changes are noted in the respective comments of each song by the editor. If instrumental accompaniments were included in the original scores, then the keyboard accompaniments in this edition are reductions of those parts. Separate obligato parts are included in the back of this book for the performance of *Ave Maria, O Come, O Come, Emmanuel* and *Panis angelicus*.

The second section of beloved folk songs and spirituals is devoted mostly to music of the United States and the British Isles, with additional titles from Israel and Mexico. These new arrangements are also introduced with editorial commentaries.

An I.P.A. Guide is provided on pages 196 and 197 of this book for reference in using the pronunciation guides. While the pronunciation guides are a helpful resource, they cannot replace the experience and expertise of a professional vocal coach or music teacher.

Singer's Library of Song is available in high, medium and low voicings, with or without compact disc recordings of the accompaniments. These accompaniments, masterfully recorded by Sally K. Albrecht, may be useful for both rehearsal and performance.

Acknowledgements

I would like to thank Jay Althouse, my editor at Alfred Music, for his excellent suggestions and thoughtful guidance in the preparation of this anthology. I would also like to express my gratitude to the following for their review of the pronunciation guides: Dr. Martha Wallen (French), Dr. David Gariff (Italian) and Ilse Hartung (Spanish) of the University of Wisconsin-Stout, Dr. Daniel Newman (German) of the University of Wisconsin-Eau Claire, Dr. Jonathan Paradise (Hebrew), Professor Emeritus of the University of Wisconsin-Minnesota and Rabbi Yosi Gordon (Hebrew). I would also like to thank Dr. Kathryn Proctor Duax of the University of Wisconsin-Eau Claire and a Vice-President of NATS for her review of the final manuscript.

Patrick M. Liebergen
March, 2005

Patrick M. Liebergen

Patrick M. Liebergen is widely published as a choral editor, arranger and composer of masterwork vocal and choral editions, collections and cantatas, as well as original choral works. The Director of Choral Activities at the University of Wisconsin-Stout in Menomonie, Wisconsin, Dr. Liebergen has served in a variety of positions as a leader of school and church music. With music degrees from St. Norbert College in DePere, WI, the University of Wisconsin-Madison, and the University of Colorado-Boulder, he frequently appears throughout the country as an adjudicator and clinician. Dr. Liebergen has received choral composition awards from the Twin Cities Church Musicians' Association, the Wisconsin Choral Directors' Association, and ASCAP, and his works have been performed by choirs around the world.

Other Vocal Books by Patrick M. Liebergen from Alfred Music

Favorite Christmas Classics for Solo Singers
Med. High Book (17923)	Book/CD (17927)
Med. Low Book (17928)	Book/CD (17930)

Favorite Sacred Classics for Solo Singers
Med. High Book (11481)	Book/CD (11511)
Med. Low Book (11482)	Book/CD (11512)

Favorite Wedding Classics for Solo Singers
Med. High Book (19898)	Book/CD (19900)
Med. Low Book (19901)	Book/CD (19903)

Sally K. Albrecht

The piano performances on the Accompaniment CDs are by Sally K. Albrecht. Sally is the Director of School Choral Publications for Alfred Music. She is a popular choral conductor, composer, and clinician, and has degrees in Music and Theater from Rollins College and an M.A. in Drama and Accompanying from the University of Miami.

Come Again, Sweet Love Doth Now Invite

John Dowland (c. 1563–1626)

John Dowland was a great English composer of songs, and a famous lutenist of his day. Early in his career, he auditioned before the Queen and was not successful in being hired in her court, possibly because of his recent conversion to Catholicism. Greatly disappointed, he left England to travel through Europe in his efforts to find performance venues. He first played his lute in Germany where he received patronage from a few benefactors, and then performed in a number of cities in Italy. In 1598 he received his first major appointment as the lutenist to King Christian IV of Denmark, where he remained until 1606. Finally returning to England, he settled in London to continue as a lutenist and composer. Although he had become well known in Europe, it wasn't until 1612 that he became employed by King Charles I.

Most of Dowland's vocal music was published in four books: *The First Booke of Songes or Ayres of foure partes with Tableture for the Lute: So made that all the partes together, or either of them severally may be song to the Lute, Orpherian or Viol de gambo* (1597); *The Second Booke of Songs or Ayres, of 2, 4, and 5 parts: With Tableture for the Lute or Orpherian, with the Violl de Gamba* (1600); *The Third and Last Booke of Songs or Aires: New Composed to sing to the Lute, Orpharion or viols (1603);* and *A Pilgrimes Solace. Wherein is contained Musicall Harmonie of 3, 4, and 5 parts to be sung and plaid with the Lute and Viols* (1612). Additionally, his music is found in the anthologies *Varieties of Lute Lessons* (1610) and *A Musicall Banquett* (1610), which were edited by his son Robert Dowland. Religion became increasingly more important to him later in his life. He therefore wrote works which were included in Thomas East's *The Whole Booke of Psalmes* (1592), and completed some spiritual songs which were included in Leighton's *The Teares or Lamentacions of a Sorrowfull Soule* (1614).

Dowland used love as the subject of many of his songs. However, other emotions are also found, such as the sadness in his "Flow My Tears" and "In Darkness Let Me Dwell." Textual declamation, the use of certain descending intervals to heighten the intensity of the more pathetic texts, and the unique marriage of poetic lines with musical phrases are some of the great achievements of Dowland's music. In comparison to the songs of his first book which have very easy rhythms and simple harmonies, the songs in his last book show a far greater use of challenging musical elements.

An innovative and creative composer, Dowland combined certain features of the secular vocal music styles and dances of his time into a new type of "lute-song," and indicated that his vocal works should be printed in a very different way. Rather than having the songs published in a set of quarto partbooks, with each book containing only the parts for one particular voice or instrument, Dowland required that all the parts of a particular song be printed on one page of a book, which was to be placed flat on a table and read by the performers gathered around it. The lute tablature was printed below the soprano part and the three lower vocal parts appeared on the page facing outwards, so that the individual members of a quartet could each read his or her part when at the table. This type of layout allowed for the song to be sung either by the solo voice alone, accompanied by a lute with or without a bass viol, or by four voices, with or without instruments, such as the lute or viols.

"Come Again, Sweet Love Doth Now Invite" was first published in Dowland's 1597 collection which premiered this new method. His first book was quite popular in its day, for it was reprinted four times. Originally scored in the key of G, this edition features modern clefs and the addition of a four measure introduction, tempo and dynamic indications and the first two of six verses provided in Dowland's manuscript. Dowland showed a great sensitivity to textual declamation in his various anthologies. The words of this song should therefore be declaimed with great care, especially emphasizing the naturally energized syllables and words.

1. Come Again, Sweet Love Doth Now Invite

from THE FIRST BOOKE OF SONGES OR AYRES
Music by **JOHN DOWLAND** (c. 1563–1626)
Edited and arranged by **PATRICK M. LIEBERGEN**

Smoothly and expressively (♩ = ca. 88)

Come a - gain, sweet love doth now in - vite Thy
gain, that I may cease to mourn Through

grac - es that re - frain To do me due de - light, To see,
thy un - kind dis - dain; For now left and for - lorn I sit,

Gioite al canto mio
(Rejoice, O Hear My Singing)

Jacopo Peri (1561–1633)

Jacopo Peri was a very significant Florentine composer of his time, completing a number of musical dramas with innovations that greatly influenced other late Renaissance and early Baroque composers. Also a singer and instrumentalist, Peri is important today for having composed *Dafne*, the first dramatic work featuring continuous music. He wrote it with the collaboration of his patron Jacopo Corsi and the poet Ottavio Rinuccini. First performed in 1598, it was among the first of its kind to be written in monodic style, which consisted of vocal solos clearly declaiming the Italian words with the support of a few instruments. This work was probably written as a result of his meeting with a group of other Renaissance poets and musicians, called the "Camerata," who were eager to revive the declamation of Greek drama. The efforts of these artists, including Giovanni de' Bardi, Giulio Caccini and Jacopo Corsi, resulted in the development of recitative and a number of music dramas.

Since most of the music of *Dafne* is lost, Peri's *Euridice*, his second collaboration with Rinuccini, is important, for the printings of this opera exist today. Completed and performed in 1600 to celebrate the marriage of Maria de' Medici and Henry IV of France, the original copies of this opera are the first published examples available of Peri's settings of narrations and dialogues for solo voices with continuo accompaniment in a dramatic format. These scores reveal that Peri's continuo part, moving slower than that of Caccini's, allows for a more parlando style of declamation by the voice.

The story of the libretto is based on the Greek myth that Orpheus, through the power of his singing, is able to gain entrance to the underworld to rescue his bride, Euridice, who had died of a snake bite. *"Gioite al canto mio"* is sung by Orpheus in the fifth and final section of this one-movement opera, when he finally returns with Euridice to the living world.

The sweeping phrases of this very joyous aria should be sung by greatly sustaining the vowels while energizing the naturally accented syllables. It was Peri's intention that the word inflections closely coincide with the rhythms of the music, and that the emotion of the words be especially heard in this new expressive style. To enhance the declamation of the text in *Euridice*, Peri did away with the Renaissance practice of independent lines, including only a singular bass part and a few indications for chordal harmonies to be sounded by a small number of instrumentalists, such as violins, recorders, harpsichord and lute. There is also evidence in his preface to *Euridice* that instruments such as the harpsichord, lira da gamba, bass lute and chitarrone played behind the scenes at the first performance. In accord with additional descriptions of early seventeenth century performances, it would be acceptable for *"Gioite al canto mio"* to be accompanied by the additional use of strings and melodic wind instruments (recorders or flutes) to enhance the sound with a discreet and simple accompaniment.

The source for this edition is the publication of Giorgio Marescotti, printed in 1600 in Florence, Italy. The note values of the original white mensural notation have been halved. The key in Marescotti's version has been retained for this edition for high voice. Modern clefs, dynamic and tempo indications, and optional English words have been included by the editor.

PRONUNCIATION GUIDE

Gio-i-te_al can-to mi-o, sel-ve fron-do-se,
dʒɔ-i-tɛ‿ɑl <u>kɑn</u>-tɔ <u>mi</u>-ɔ, <u>sɛl</u>-vɛ frɔn-<u>do</u>-zɛ,

Gio-i-te_a-ma-ti col-li, e-d'o-gn'in-tor-no,
dʒɔ-i-tɛ‿ɑ-<u>mɑ</u>-ti <u>kɔl</u>ːli ɛ-<u>do</u>-ɲin-<u>tor</u>-nɔ,

Ec-co rim-bom-bi dal-le val-li_a-sco-se.
ɛ - kɔ rim-<u>bom</u>-bi <u>dɑl</u>ːlɛ <u>vɑl</u>ːli‿ɑ-s<u>ko</u>-zɛ.

Ri-sor-to_è'l mio bel sol di rag-gi_a-dor-no,
ri - <u>sor</u>-tɔ‿ɛl miɔ bɛl sol di <u>rɑd</u>ːdʒi‿ɑ-<u>dor</u>-nɔ,

E co' be-gl'oc-chi, on-de fa scor-no_a De-lo,
ɛ kɔ be-<u>ʎɔk</u>ːki,   on-dɛ fɑ s<u>kor</u>-nɔ‿ɑ <u>dɛ</u>-lɔ,

Rad-dop-pia fo-co_a l'al-me, e lu-ce _ al gior-no,
rɑdːdopːpjɑ <u>fɔ</u>-kɔ‿ɑlːlɑl-mɛ,‿e <u>lu</u>-tʃɛ‿ɑl dʒor-nɔ,

E fa ser-vi d'a-mor la ter-ra_e'l Cie-lo.
e fɑ <u>sɛr</u>-vi dɑ - <u>mor</u> lɑ <u>tɛr</u>ːrɑ‿el tʃɛ-lɔ.

Footnotes to Italian Pronunciation

- In multiple syllable words, the syllables that should be stressed are underlined.

- [ɲ] indicates that the tip of the tongue should be in contact with the lower front teeth while the front of the tongue is raised and pressed against the front of the hard palate. Nasality is then produced when breath passes through the nose.

- [r] should be trilled in the performance of this song.

- [ʎ] indicates a similar sound to [lj] in the word "million"—[mɪ-ljən], requiring only one tongue action, as in the word "giglio"—[dʒi-ʎɔ].

- Certain double consonants can be sustained on a pitch while maintaining a legato line, such as those in the words "colli" and "valli." The singer should take time for the singable double consonants in each of these words from the preceding musical note.

- There are other double consonants, such as those in the words "raggi" and "occhi," which interrupt the legato line when pronounced correctly. For example, when singing the word "raggi" [rɑdːdʒi], the singer should briefly stop on the [d], creating a slight silence before the sounding of the [dʒ].

TRANSLATION

Rejoice at my song, leafy woods,
Rejoice, beloved hills and from all around
May the echo resound from the hidden valleys.
Resurrected is my beautiful sun adored with rays,
And with beautiful eyes, which makes scorn to Delos,
She redoubles fire to souls and light to the day,
And makes Heaven and earth the servants of love.

2. Gioite al canto mio

(Rejoice, O Hear My Singing)

Italian words by
OTTAVIO RINUCCINI (1562–1612)
English words by **PATRICK M. LIEBERGEN**

from EURIDICE
Music by **JACOPO PERI** (1561–1633)
Arranged by **PATRICK M. LIEBERGEN**

Ave Maria

Giulio Caccini (1545–1618)

Giulio Caccini was a highly successful song composer as well as a singer, voice teacher and instrumentalist in Italy in the early part of the Baroque era. His musical career began in Rome, where he was employed as a singer in the Cappela Giulia. He was later recruited to work in Florence, where he remained to sing, teach and compose music for the Medici court entertainment and sacred services.

In Florence, his composition of songs was greatly influenced by a group of intellectuals, professional artists and high respected amateurs, which became known as the "Camerata." This group met at the home of Count Bardi to discuss the revival of the Greek dramatic style.

Caccini eventually became famous for developing this new style of solo song, which involved a declamatory setting of the words, a musical sensitivity to the structure of the text, and a flexible approach to rhythm and tempo. This new type of song, called monody, included the performance of ornaments written out on the score, accompanied by a simple basso continuo. Since the bass part was to be harmonized in an improvisatory manner on another instrument, Caccini included a shorthand method of figures on the score to indicate which harmonies were to be played.

Caccini published his first collection of songs, *Le nuove musiche*, in 1602 and his second collection, *Nuove musiche e nuova maniera di scriverle*, in 1614. His first publication consisted of madrigals and airs for solo voice with basso continuo that he had written in the previous twenty years of his life. It was in the preface of this historically significant collection that he described the important characteristics of this new monodic style.

Caccini's beautiful *"Ave Maria"* has become one of his most beloved solo works in recent years.

PRONUNCIATION GUIDE

A-ve Ma-ri-a. A-men.
ɑː-ʋɛ mɑ-<u>ri</u>ː-ɑ. ɑ-mɛn.

Footnotes to Latin Pronunciation

• The syllables that should be stressed are underlined.

• [ɾ] should be flipped.

TRANSLATION

Hail Mary. Amen

The optional flute part for this arrangement is found on pages 190 and 191.

This arrangement is available for performance by S.A.T.B. (21042), T.T.B.B. (22963), S.A.B. (20143) and 2-part (20144) voices, published by Alfred Music.

3. Ave Maria

Text setting and Arrangement by
PATRICK M. LIEBERGEN

Music attributed to
GIULIO CACCINI (1545–1618)

Flute part is on page 190.

men.   A - men.

poco rit.

dim. poco a poco

poco rit.

I Attempt from Love's Sickness

Henry Purcell (1659–1695)

Beloved by the English people and recognized as a genius in his own lifetime, Henry Purcell was a highly talented Baroque composer and one of the greatest English composers of all time. Beginning his musical experiences as a chorister in the Chapel Royal, Purcell had quite a varied and successful career. He was appointed composer to the King in 1677 and the organist of Westminster Abbey in 1679. He served in his church music position until his death, providing music for the coronation of two English kings and for the funeral of Queen Mary. He also contributed to the 1694 edition of Playford's instruction book titled *An Introduction to the Skill of Musick* and wrote music for theatrical productions in the latter portion of his life.

His greatness can be seen in the large number and variety of works of the highest quality which he wrote during his short life of only 36 years. Besides many odes and welcome songs for chorus and orchestra, cantatas, songs, catches, anthems, services, fancies, chamber sonatas, keyboard works and a variety of other instrumental pieces, he wrote several semi-operas and incidental music for numerous plays. His *Dido and Aeneas* was the first great English opera.

Beginning in 1690 until his death, Purcell became quite involved in writing for the operatic market, for success in the theatre gave him a much higher income than the occasional performances of his odes, welcome songs and anthems. Completing his semi-operas and providing incidental music for plays resulted in increased sales of his music in print.

"I Attempt from Love's Sickness" is a lively song from the semi-opera *The Indian Queen* (z 630), Purcell's largest stage project in 1695. For his last music drama, Purcell chose an improbable story, from a play with the same name, which was the collaboration of John Dryden and his brother-in-law, Sir Robert Howard. The plot involves a theme of war between Peru and Mexico and also love relationships between individuals in the Inca and Aztec empires. Set in six acts, it is in the third act that the Spirits of the Air encourage Zempoalla, queen of the Mexicans, to forget her love for the Peruvian General Montezuma. Zempoalla acknowledges her incapacity to escape with the singing of "I Attempt from Love's Sickness."

Originally scored for high voice and continuo only, this edition is in the original key and includes the addition of the four measure introduction and a keyboard accompaniment adapted from the original continuo part. Modern clefs and tempo and dynamic indications have also been added.

Although "I Attempt from Love's Sickness" is performed by a soprano in a performance of *The Indian Queen*, this solo is an excellent choice for singers of other voice classifications, for it enables singers to work on vocal technique and to experience the style of a truly gifted composer of Baroque music.

4. I Attempt from Love's Sickness

Words by **ROBERT HOWARD** (1626–1698)
and **JOHN DRYDEN** (1631–1700)

from THE INDIAN QUEEN
Music by **HENRY PURCELL** (1659–1695)
Edited by **PATRICK M. LIEBERGEN**

I at-tempt from love's sick-ness to fly___ in___

vain, Since I am my-self my own fe-ver, since I am my-

tempt from love's— sick - ness to fly———————————————————— in—

vain, Since I am my - self my own fe - ver, since

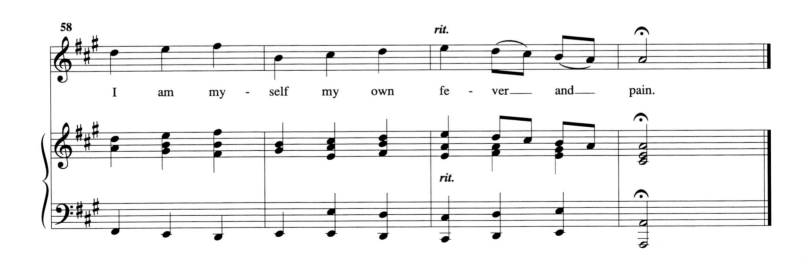

I am my - self my own fe - ver— and— pain.

Bois épais
(Gloomy Woods)

Jean-Baptiste Lully (1632–1687)

Jean-Baptiste Lully was a leading musician in France during the Baroque era and the founder of French opera. Born in Florence, Italy, Lully was taken to Paris early in his life because of his beautiful singing voice. Working at first as a page in a royal family, his musical talents were soon developed, and he became a successful composer, dancer and violinist. Because of his exceptional musical ability and tremendous ambition, Lully became quite powerful in the musical venues of Paris, composing music for ballets and theatrical productions as well as conducting orchestras and choral presentations. Becoming a naturalized French citizen brought him a great amount of royal favor. His numerous musical successes led to his conducting and composing in the court of Louis XIV.

Lully wrote a number of motets, secular vocal pieces and instrumental works in addition to his very important music for the theater. He became especially famous for his work in operas, in which he replaced the Italian recitativo secco with recitatives that had accompaniments and proper text accentuations for the French language. He developed the operatic overture to a new degree of importance, establishing the French overture with three contrasting slow-fast-slow movements. He elevated the standard of orchestral performance to a far greater level than had previously been accomplished in the court. Lully also wrote ballets incorporating quicker dances, and he established the tradition of French opera, sometimes more specifically called *tragédies lyriques*.

Lully is often remembered today for the manner of his death. While conducting a performance of his *Te Deum* by pounding a pole on the floor, he accidentally hit his foot and died three months later from an infection.

"Bois épais" is a tragic aria from Lully's opera *Amadis*, which was premiered in Paris in 1684. The libretto by Philippe Quinault portrays Amadis, the main character, as a great French hero who is without weakness. The main theme of this drama is the love of Amadis and Orianne, although various events and characters are freely interwoven in this medieval romance of love and glory.

This edition of Amadis's solo has been transposed down a perfect fourth from the original. The keyboard part provided in this edition is a reduction of the original string and continuo parts. Additionally, the original instrumental introduction of fourteen measures labeled "Prélude" has been replaced with a shorter keyboard introduction. Tempo and dynamic indications and the English words have also been added by the editor.

On certain notes, the "t" indication that appears in the original score to indicate a trill has also been included in this publication. While it is acceptable to sing this piece without sounding any trill, today's singer may wish to perform this type of ornamentation which was extensively practiced by the musicians of the French Baroque at cadence points. A Baroque trill should start on the upper note, whether preceded by that note or not. The upper note, called the appoggiatura, should be lengthened with expressive stress before the rest of the trill is sounded.

PRONUNCIATION GUIDE

Bois é - pais, re-dou-ble ton om-bre,
bwa ze-p<u>ɛ</u>, ɾə-<u>du</u> - blə tɔ̃ n<u>ɔ̃</u>-bɾə,

Tu ne sau-rais ê-tre_as-sez som-bre,
ty nə sɔ - <u>ɾɛ</u> zɛ tɾɑ-<u>se</u> s<u>ɔ̃</u> - bɾə,

Tu ne peux trop ca-cher mon mal-heu-reux a - mour.
ty nə pø tro kɑ-<u>ʃe</u> mɔ̃ mɑ-lœ-<u>ɾø</u> zɑ-<u>muɾ</u>.

Je sens un dés-es-poir dont l'hor-reur est ex-trê - me,
ʒə sɑ̃ zœ̃ de-zɛ-<u>spwɑɾ</u> dɔ̃ lɔ <u>ɾœ</u> - ɾɛ tɛ-<u>kstɾɛ</u>-mə,

Je ne dois plus voir ce que j'ai-me,
ʒə nə dwɑ ply vwɑɾ sə kə <u>ʒɛ</u> - mə,

Je ne veux plus souf-frir le jour.
ʒə nə vø ply su - <u>fɾiɾ</u> lə ʒuɾ.

Footnotes to French Pronunciation

• In multiple syllable words, the syllables that should be stressed are underlined.

• [ɾ] should be flipped.

• [˜] indicates that the vowel below it should be nasalized.

TRANSLATION

Thick woods, increase your shade,
You could not be dark enough,
You are not able to hide my unhappy love too much.
I feel a despair whose horror is extreme,
I am no longer to see what I love,
I no longer want to suffer the day.

5. Bois épais
(Gloomy Woods)

French words by
PHILIPPE QUINAULT (1635–1688)
English words by **PATRICK M. LIEBERGEN**

from **AMADIS DE GAULE**
Music by **JEAN-BAPTISTE LULLY** (1632–1687)
Edited by **PATRICK M. LIEBERGEN**

Bois é - pais re - dou - ble ton om - bre,
Gloom - y woods, so dark, thick - ly shad - ed,

Tu ne sau - rais ê - tre as-sez som - bre, Tu ne peux trop ca -
Deep in the for - est light is fad - ed. The dark - ness hides my

Jesu, Joy of Man's Desiring

Johann Sebastian Bach (1685–1750)

Johann Sebastian Bach was a musical genius who lived at the end of the Baroque era. Recognized as one of the greatest composers of all time, he wrote in almost every musical genre of his time and was especially successful at contrapuntal technique.

Born into a large family of musicians, Bach spent his entire life in the Thuringia area of Germany. After early training in organ and violin, he performed as an organist in Arnstadt and Mülhausen. During his subsequent assignment as court organist and chamber musician to the Duke of Weimar, Bach wrote most of his finest organ works and a number of sacred and secular works. Moving to Cöthen, he wrote his chief orchestral and chamber music works as Kapellmeister and Director of Chamber Music for the Prince of Anhalt.

In 1722, Bach was appointed Cantor at St. Thomas' Church in Leipzig, where he spent his remaining years composing most of his great church music. It was in Leipzig that he completed the majority of his chorale cantatas, which were required for use in the Lutheran worship services and other occasions. Bach's chorale cantatas typically incorporated Lutheran chorale tunes in settings for soloists, choir and orchestra. Their texts were usually adapted from the Bible, the Lutheran service, and hymns or chorales.

Bach was a master at combining the music and words of a cantata to highlight the scriptural texts and sermon themes prescribed for certain days.

The famous melody known as "Jesu, Joy of Man's Desiring" appears in the sixth and tenth movements of Bach's Cantata No. 147, *Herz und Mund und Tat und Leben*. Written for the Feast of the Visitation, the cantata was first performed in Leipzig on July 2, 1723. In it, Bach set Johann Schop's chorale melody using different verses of Martin Jahn's German text of 1661 for the two movements. Bach scored the movements for S.A.T.B. voices with trumpet, strings and continuo as accompaniment. This arrangement of the melody for high voice is a whole step higher than the original key and includes a keyboard accompaniment fashioned by the editor from Bach's orchestral parts. The editor has also provided tempo and dynamic indications.

In performance, the very joyful message of the text should be conveyed by legato singing, and the tempo should remain constant throughout the work, with a slight ritardando just before the end of the piece. The first verse may be sung at Christmas or at other times during the year. In the spirit of Bach, the editor has provided an alternate second verse which may be sung during Advent.

6. Jesu, Joy of Man's Desiring

Verse 1 by **ROBERT BRIDGES**
Verse 2 by **PATRICK M. LIEBERGEN**

from Cantata No. 147 *Herz und Mund und Tat und Leben*
Music by **JOHANN SEBASTIAN BACH** (1685–1750)
Edited and arranged by **PATRICK M. LIEBERGEN**

Je - su, joy of man's de -
Son of God with joy a -

Soar to un- cre- at- ed_____
We a- wait your guid- ing_____

light.
light.

Word of God, our flesh_____ that fash- ion'd,
All re- joice with grate- ful sing- ing,

throne.
love.

Bist du bei mir

(If You're with Me)
as found in the **1725 Notebook of Anna Magdalena Bach**

Gottfried Heinrich Stölzel (1690-1749)

This well-known melody from Anna Magdalena's notebook has often been attributed to her husband, Johann Sebastian Bach (1685–1750). However, the melody, bass line and German text were probably written by Gottfried Heinrich Stölzel. A German composer and theorist, Stölzel was highly regarded in his lifetime for his numerous musical accomplishments.

Stölzel's musical education began early in his life through private instruction and attendance at Leipzig University. Numerous trips through Germany and other countries on music assignments put him in contact with some of the outstanding composers of his time, such as Vivaldi and Scarlatti. After completing a number of commissioned works, he finally settled at the court at Saxe-Gothe, where he held the appointment of Kapellmeister for thirty years. It was there that he wrote music for the church, opera and court festivities. He continued to fulfill commissions while in that position and was regarded as a superb teacher and theorist. In addition, he wrote the first significant treatise on recitative.

Anna Magdalena Wilcken Bach (1701-1760) became the second wife of Johann Sebastian Bach in 1721 after his first wife died. An excellent soprano who had been employed at the Cöthen court, she was responsible for copying much of her husband's music. He also instructed her in the art of playing figured bass. In 1725, he presented her with a notebook so that she could fill it with music of various kinds, including preludes, suites, chorales, and sacred and secular songs.

"*Bist du bei mir*" is found in this notebook. Only the German words, melody and bass line of this song are provided. To this framework, the editor has added a realization of the original music, an English version, and suggestions for tempo and dynamics. This version is presented one half step lower than the original key.

PRONUNCIATION GUIDE

Bist du bei mir, geh' ich mit Freu-den,
bɪst du baɪ miːɾ, geː ɪç mɪt fɾɔʏ-dən,

zum Ster-ben und zu mei-ner Ruh',
tsum ʃtɛɾ-bən ʊnt tsu maɪ-nəɾ ɾuː,

zum Ster-ben und zu   mei-ner Ruh'.
tsum ʃtɛɾ-bən ʊnt tsu: maɪ-nəɾ ɾuː.

Ach, wie ver-gnügt wär so mein En-de,
ɑx,   viː fɛɾ-gnyːkt vɛːɾ zo maɪn ɛn-də,

es drück-ten dei-ne schö-nen Hän-de
ɛs dɾʏk - tən daɪ-nə ʃø - nən hɛn-də

mir die ge-treu-en Au-gen zu.
miɾ di gə-tɾɔʏ-ən ɑʊ-gən tsu.

Footnotes to German Pronunciation

- In multiple syllable words, the syllables that should be stressed are underlined.

- [ɾ] should be flipped.

TRANSLATION

If you are with me,
I will gladly go to my death and my rest.
Ah, how pleasant will be my end,
if your dear hands will close my faithful eyes shut.

7. Bist du bei mir

(If You're with Me)

English words by
PATRICK M. LIEBERGEN

from the 1725 Notebook of
ANNA MAGDALENA BACH*
Edited and arranged by **PATRICK M. LIEBERGEN**

*Melody, bass line and German text probably were probably written by Gottfried Heinrich Stölzel (1690–1749).

Where'er You Walk

George Frideric Handel (1685-1759)

George Frideric Handel was a renowned composer of instrumental and vocal works at the end of the Baroque era. Born in Halle, Germany, he took music lessons with Friedrich Wilhelm Zachau, and served as assistant organist at Halle Cathedral before moving to Hamburg to pursue his musical career. While in Hamburg he became a violinist in the opera house orchestra and composed his first opera, *Almira*. Handel, then visited Italy in 1706 to learn the Italian style of composition, completing a number of successful operas as well as cantatas and instrumental music. After additional international travel, he eventually settled in England to become a leading musical figure as a composer of operas and oratorios, although he wrote a number of beloved instrumental pieces, such as *Water Music*, and ceremonial church music.

Handel became tremendously successful in England from the very beginning of his musical endeavors there. *Rinaldo*, his first opera for the people of London, was hailed as a great success, and subsequent works when he was a young man in his twenties brought him tremendous notoriety. Eventually becoming a leading figure in London's musical life, Handel was honored by both Queen Anne and King George I with financial backing and honors for his musical successes. His large-scale oratorios in English, including many exuberant choruses for the people, made him especially popular in England. Over 3000 persons attended Handel's funeral in Westminster Abbey.

"Where'er You Walk" is from Handel's *Semele*. *Semele* was composed by Handel as a secular presentation meant to be presented on stage by soloists and a chorus without dramatic action. The libretto of *Semele* was the work of the esteemed British dramatist William Congreve, who originally called his work "an opera" when it was first published in 1707. However, its lack of dramatic qualities resulted in no composer using it until Handel decided to compose music based on a revision of Congreve's original work. Beginning the piece on June 3, 1743, Handel completed it in merely one month for presentation in the manner of an oratorio. Its premiere was quite unsuccessful to a large crowd on February 10, 1744 at the oratorio festival at Covent Garden. Although Handel subsequently reworked the score in an effort to improve the work, it never gained popularity and was never revived in Handel's lifetime.

The story of *Semele* is mythological and is a very involved story of the love relationships of many characters. Handel enjoyed setting the music in the spirit of the content, based on the theme of love. Although the work was unsuccessful for Handel and is rarely performed today, the music contains moments of great beauty. One memorable melody is that of "Where'er You Walk," an aria sung by Jupiter, a tenor soloist, in the Second Act. This melody is masterfully woven together between the solo and instrumental parts in Handel's setting.

Handel originally scored this solo with an accompaniment of first and second violins, viola and continuo in the key of B-flat major. This edition provides a keyboard part based on the original instrumental parts. Tempo and dynamic indications are further additions to Handel's original score.

8. Where'er You Walk

Words by **WILLIAM CONGREVE** (1670–1729)

from SEMELE
Music by **GEORGE FRIDERIC HANDEL** (1685–1759)
Edited by **PATRICK M. LIEBERGEN**

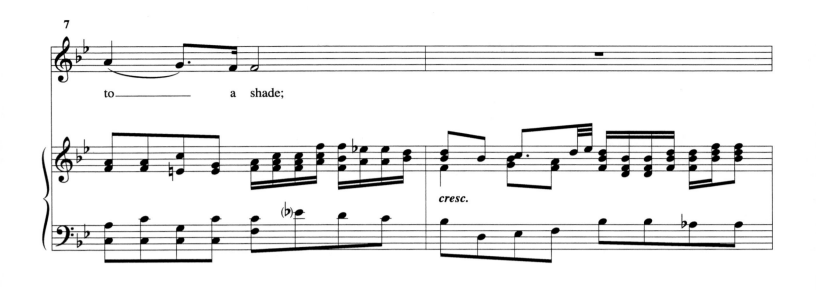

to _____ a shade;

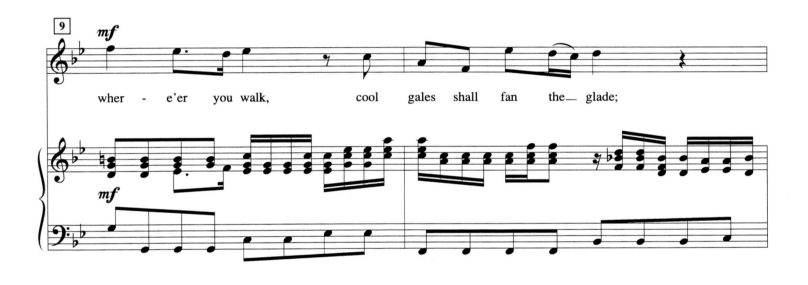

wher - e'er you walk, cool gales shall fan the_ glade;

trees, where you sit, shall crowd in - to a_ shade, _____

trees, where you sit,

shall crowd in - to a shade.

Wher - e'er you_ tread, the blush - ing flow'rs shall rise, and

all things flour - ish, and all things flour - ish wher -

e'er you turn your eyes, wher - e'er you turn your eyes, wher - e'er you turn your eyes.

Where'er You Walk ■ 47

Wiegenlied
(Lullaby)

Johannes Brahms (1833-1897)

Johannes Brahms was one of the greatest composers of the nineteenth century. Besides 190 solo lieder and additional songs for various vocal combinations, he published seven volumes of folk song arrangements, six works for chorus and orchestra, *German Requiem*, four symphonies, two concert overtures, two piano concertos, three string quartets, and a variety of selections for solo piano and chamber music pieces. Many of his works reveal his reverence for the music of the old masters, from the Renaissance onwards. Rather than discarding the compositional techniques of the past for something new, he infused those techniques with the established forms into his own style of romanticism.

Born in Hamburg and receiving music education early in his life, he soon became an accomplished pianist. When he left home as a young man to accompany a violinist in a few towns in Germany, he met a number of important musical figures, including Robert and Clara Schumann. They instantly recognized his talent as a young composer, and his long friendship with the Schumanns greatly influenced his tremendously successful career. Both Robert and Clara encouraged him to compose, promoting his abilities and introducing him to important figures. Brahms's early career involved conducting choirs and traveling to conduct his works. Brahms finally settled in Vienna to conduct the orchestra and chorus of the *Gessellschaft der Musikfreunde*. He eventually became the dominant musical figure in Vienna the last twenty years of his life, receiving medals and honors while achieving continued success as a composer and conductor of his own works.

Brahms's "*Wiegenlied*," from Opus 49, is one of the best-loved of all his songs. Its first verse comes from the fifteenth century text found in *Des Knaben Wunderhorn,* an anthology of German folk poems collected by Achim von Armin and Clemens von Brentano, published in 1805–1808. Brahms showed reverence for his Germanic heritage throughout his career, often turning to anthologies of anonymous texts in setting his songs. The words of the second verse of "*Wiegenlied*" were later added by Georg Scherer.

Brahms also borrowed musical material in setting "*Wiegenlied*." He used a folk song melody from the collection of Kretzschmer and Zuccamaglio titled *Deutsche Volkslieder mit ihren Original-Weisen.* Employing a tuneful vocal line from that collection, Brahms achieved a rocking motion by using elements of an upper Austrian waltz song.

"*Wiegenlied*" was composed to honor the second child, Hans, of his friends Bertha and Artus Faber. Brahms sent the song to the Fabers with the note that it was meant for Bertha to sing to Hans in helping the child fall asleep. This now famous tune is known as the "Brahms Lullaby."

Originally set in E-flat major, this version has been transposed up one step for high voice. A metronomic indication and additional dynamics have been added to the original score.

In measures 15 and 33, the grace note should be sounded as an eighth note and the half note in those measures should be shortened to a dotted quarter note as follows:

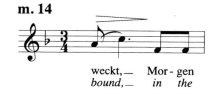

In measures 18 and 36, the two grace notes which appear together as an ornamentation should be treated as two sixteenth notes, resulting in a rhythm on the first beat of each measure as follows:

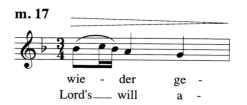

PRONUNCIATION GUIDE

Wiegenlied
vigənlit

Gu-ten A-bend, gut' Nacht,
gu-tən a-bənt   gut naxt,

mit Ro-sen be-dacht,
mıt ro-zən bə-daxt,

mit Näg'-lein be-steckt,
mıt neːg-laın bə-ʃtɛkt,

schlupf' un-ter die Deck'.
ʃlʊpf   ʊn-təɾ di dɛk.

Mor-gen früh, wenn Gott will,
mɔɾ-gən fɾy   vɛn gɔt vıl,

wirst du wie-der ge-weckt.
vıɾst du vi - dəɾ gə-vɛkt.

Gu-ten A-bend, gut' Nacht,
gu -tən a-bənt   gut naxt,

von Eng'-lein be-wacht,
fɔn ɛŋ - laın bə-vaxt,

die zei - gen im Traum
di   tsaı-gən ım traʊm

dir Christ-kind-leins Baum:
diɾ kɾıst - kınt-laıns baʊm:

Schlaf' nun se-lig und süss,
ʃlaf   nun ze-lıç ʊnt zʏs,

schau' im Traum's Pa-ra-dies.
ʃaʊ   ım traʊmz pa-ɾa-dis.

Footnotes to German Pronunciation

• In multiple syllable words, the vowels that should be stressed are underlined.

• [ɾ] should be flipped.

TRANSLATION

Good evening, good night,
with roses covering you,
with little pinks adorning you,
slip under the blanket.
Tomorrow morning, if God wills,
you will awaken again.

Good evening, good night,
watched over by little angels,
who show you in the dream
the little Christ-child's tree:
sleep now blissfully and sweetly,
see Paradise in your dreams.

9. Wiegenlied
(Lullaby)

German words from DES KNABEN WUNDERHORN, 1808 (first stanza)
and second stanza by **GEORG SCHERER** (1824–1909)
English words by **PATRICK M. LIEBERGEN**

Op. 49, No. 4
Music by **JOHANNES BRAHMS** (1833–1897)
Edited by **PATRICK M. LIEBERGEN**

*Zart bewegt: Gently animated

wie - der ge - weckt,   Mor - gen früh,   wenn Gott will,   Wirst du
Lord's   will   a -   bound,   in the   morn -   ing   a - wake,   may the

wie - der ge - weckt.   Gu - ten
Lord's — will   a -   bound.   *Go   to*

A - bend, gut' Nacht,   von — Eng' - lein be - wacht, —   die —
sleep   and good   night,   the — an - gels   de - light, —   now —

zei - gen im___ Traum dir___ Christ - kind - leins Baum: Schlaf' nun
dream through the___ night, your___ Christ - child in - vite, Go to

se - lig und süss, schau' im Traum's Pa - ra - dies, Schlaf' nun
sleep and be blest, par - a - dise in your rest, go to

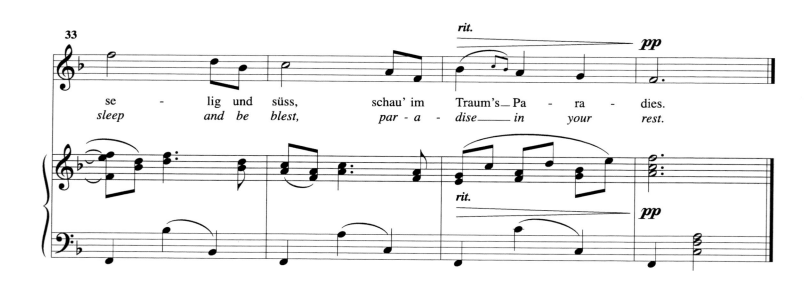

se - lig und süss, schau' im Traum's Pa - ra - dies.
sleep and be blest, par - a - dise___ in your rest.

Love Has Eyes

Henry R. Bishop (1786–1855)

Henry R. Bishop was a very popular conductor and composer of opera in England in the early part of the nineteenth century. Revered in his day for his adaptations of beloved operas, such as Mozart's *Le nozze di Figaro* and Rossini's *Il barbiere di Siviglia*, Bishop also completed numerous original operas and a variety of vocal pieces for groups and individual soloists.

Bishop began his career by writing dramatic works and ballets for the King's Theatre and Drury Lane Theatre in London. He was appointed the composer and musical director at Covent Garden in 1810, and became especially successful in providing theatrical entertainments. He left Covent Garden in 1824 because of a dispute in his salary, thereafter continuing to work at Drury Lane and finally Vauxhall Gardens through 1840. Bishop did not write very much music in his latter years. Instead, he edited music of the masters from the Baroque era and became a professor of music at Edinburgh and eventually at Oxford. Also interested in instrumental music, he founded the Philharmonic Society in 1813, for which he conducted several concerts, and traveled on the mainland to conduct. Bishop was quite influential, for he kept the English opera alive in London and wrote some very memorable melodies. He was the first musician to be knighted by a British monarch.

Bishop's most famous song is "Home, Sweet Home." It was first published in 1821 as a "Sicilian air" in a collection of melodies titled *National Airs*. The melody was used again in 1823 as the theme song of *Clairi, The Maid of Milan*, an opera which was set to the famous words of the American poet John Howard Payne. This folk-like tune is found in many songbooks and is highly revered to this day in Europe and America.

Another favorite ballad which has been included in a number of vocal anthologies is "Love Has Eyes," a very energetic song performed by Captain Belton in Bishop's comic opera *The Farmer's Wife*. Published in 1814, this opera of three acts with libretto by Charles Dibdin was first performed at the Treatre Royal, Covent Garden.

Bishop's original indications, such as staccato, slur, trill, fermata and tempo, are included in this edition. The editor has replaced Bishop's indications of *rinformzando (rf)* with the indications of *sforzando*. The terms are synonymous, for they call for a note or a chord to be suddenly accented. Additionally, metronomic and dynamic indications have been added to Bishop's original version. Bishop set this solo for high voice with piano accompaniment in B-flat major. This version is transposed down one whole step to make it more accessible for a high voice.

10. Love Has Eyes

Words by **CHARLES DIBDIN** (1745–1814)

from THE FARMER'S WIFE
Music by **HENRY R. BISHOP** (1786–1855)
Edited by **PATRICK M. LIEBERGEN**

Love's blind they say,_____

Oh nev- er nay,_____ Can words love's_ grace_ im - part?_____ The

*Scherzando: Playful

love has eyes! Oh,— yes be-lieve— me, Oh,— yes be-lieve— me,

Oh,— yes be-lieve— me,— love—— has eyes!——

Love's wing'd they cry,—— Oh, nev-er I,—— No pin-ions—

Heidenröslein
(Little Heath-Rose)

Franz Schubert (1797-1828)

Franz Schubert was born in Vienna and began his musical education early in life, studying violin, piano, organ, singing and theory. In 1808, he became a member of the Court Chapel Choir and also studied music at the Stadkonvict, a training school for court singers. Upon leaving Stadkonvict, he spent a year training as a teacher to be employed in his father's school. With many works written and numerous contacts made with other musicians in Vienna, he eventually left his teaching position to spend the rest of his life composing music. Like Mozart, he suffered from the lack of secure patronage and a steady income. Schubert composed an incredible amount of music in his brief life of only thirty-one years.

Included in Schubert's works are nine symphonies, twenty-two piano sonatas, many short piano pieces for two and four hands, thirty-five chamber works, six masses, seventeen operas and over 600 songs, including his two song cycles *Die schöne Müllerin* and *Winterreise*. Although his piano, chamber and orchestral works are important contributions to music literature, his songs are especially revered today for their beauty and genius.

Schubert was the first major composer to devote a considerable amount of his creative work to writing songs. *"Hagars Klage,"* his first song, was written in 1811 when he was only fourteen years old. By the time Schubert left school at 16 years old, he had already written a great amount of music. 1815 was an exceptional year for Schubert's productivity, when he wrote about 140 songs, completing as many as eight lieder (songs) in one day. Many of them were settings of the celebrated poet, Johann Wolfgang von Goethe.

Schubert's settings of Goethe's texts in 1815 included the beloved ballad *"Heidenröslein"* and *"Erlkönig,"* a dramatic narrative depicting a father's ride through the night while trying to save his child from the King of the Elves. The tremendous success of *"Erlkönig"* at a concert in 1821 led to the publication of his songs and to financial independence. Although *"Erlkönig"* was Schubert's most famous song in the nineteenth century, his financial success was short-lived, and he struggled in the latter years of his life with financial and health problems.

With a gift for writing beautiful and tuneful melodies, Schubert unified poetry and music in a very creative way. He used the piano as an expressive instrument to blend the voice and text, and he was especially successful at capturing the mood of a poem, using verse that could convey the meaning. Besides the texts of Schiller, Klopstock, Heine, Müller and Rückert, Goethe's poems were well represented throughout the lifelong work of Schubert. Goethe was significant for introducing a new lyricism in German poetry, full of personal expression and awareness of self.

Goethe originally wrote the words of *"Heidenröslein"* to fit a folk tune dating back to the sixteenth century. Those words were used in a 1793 setting for solo voice and keyboard by Johann Friedrich Reichardt. Schubert later set Goethe's poem with an original melody in the spirit of the folk song tradition and resembling the gracefulness of Mozart. Schubert's *"Heidenröslein"* was composed in G major, and was published by Cappi and Diabelli as Op. 3, No. 3 in May, 1821. It is listed as D. 257.

PRONUNCIATION GUIDE

Stanza 1

Sah ein Knab' ein Rös-lein stehn,
zɑː ain knap ain ˈrøs-laɪn ʃteːn,

Rös-lein auf der Hei-den,
ˈrøs-laɪn ɑʊf deɾ ˈhaɪ- dən,

war so jung und mor-gen-schön,
vɑɾ zo juŋ ʊnt ˈmɔɾ-gən-ʃøn,

lief er schnell, es nah zu sehn,
lif eːɾ ʃnɛl,   ɛs nɑː tsu zeːn,

sah's mit vie-len Freu-den.
zɑːs mɪt ˈfil-ən ˈfɾɔʏ-dən.

Rös-lein, Rös-lein, Rös-lein rot,
ˈrøs-laɪn, ˈrøs-laɪn, ˈrøs-laɪn rot,

Rös-lein auf der Hei-den.
ˈrøs-laɪn ɑʊf deɾ ˈhaɪ-dən.

Stanza 2

Kna-be sprach: ich bre-che dich,
ˈknɑ-bə ʃpɾɑx, ɪç ˈbɾɛ-çə dɪç,

Rös-lein auf der Hei-den,
ˈrøs-laɪn ɑʊf deɾ ˈhaɪ- dən,

Rös-lein sprach: ich ste-che dich,
ˈrøs-laɪn ʃpɾɑx   ɪç ˈstɛ-çə dɪç,

dass du e-wig denkst an mich,
das du ˈe-vɪç dɛŋkst an mɪç,

und ich will's nicht lei-den.
ʊnt ɪç vɪls nɪçt ˈlaɪ-dən.

Rös-lein, Rös-lein, Rös-lein rot,
ˈrøs- laɪn, ˈrøs-laɪn, ˈrøs-laɪn rot,

Rös-lein auf der Hei-den.
ˈrøs-laɪn ɑʊf deɾ ˈhaɪ- dən.

Stanza 3

Und der wil-de Kna-be brach's
ʊnt der ˈvɪl-də ˈknɑː-bə bɾɑxs

Rös-lein auf der Hei-den,
ˈrøs-laɪn ɑʊf deɾ ˈhaɪ- dən,

Rös-lein wehr-te sich und stach,
ˈrøs-laɪn veːɾ - tə zɪç ʊnt ʃtɑx,

half ihm doch kein Weh und Ach,
half iːm dɔx kaɪn veː ʊnt ax,

musst es e-ben lei-den.
mʊst ɛs ˈe-bən ˈlaɪ-dən.

Rös-lein, Rös-lein, Rös-lein rot,
ˈrøs- laɪn, ˈrøs-laɪn, ˈrøs-laɪn ɾot,

Rös-lein auf der Hei-den.
ˈrøs-laɪn ɑʊf deɾ ˈhaɪ- dən.

Footnotes to German Pronunciation

• In multiple syllable words, the vowels that should be stressed are underlined.

• [ɾ] should be flipped.

TRANSLATION

A boy saw a little rose standing,
Little rose in the heather,
It was so young and morning-beautiful,
He quickly ran closer to see it,
He saw it with many joys.
Little rose, little rose, little rose red,
Little rose in the heather.

Said the boy: I will pluck you,
Little rose in the heather,
Said the little rose: I will prick you,
So that you will always think of me,
And I will not suffer it.
Little rose, Little rose, Little rose red,
Little rose in the heather.

And the wild boy plucked
The little rose in the heather;
The little rose defended itself and pricked him,
However no cries of pain helped it,
It just had to suffer.
Little rose, little rose, little rose red,
Little rose in the heather.

11. Heidenröslein

(Little Heath-Rose)

German words by
JOHANN WOLFGANG VON GOETHE (1749–1832)
English words by **PATRICK M. LIEBERGEN**

Op. 3, No. 3
Music by **FRANZ SCHUBERT** (1797–1828)
Edited by **PATRICK M. LIEBERGEN**

*Lieblich: Lovely

Die Lotosblume
(The Lotus Flower)

Robert Schumann (1810–1856)

Robert Schumann was a great German composer and one of the most important figures of the Romantic period. Most revered for his piano music and songs, he also wrote an opera, choral works, symphonies and concert overtures.

Born into a family involved with publishing and selling books, Robert Schumann was introduced from his very early years to both literature and music. While in the home of his parents, Schumann read many of the classics of literature and began piano lessons, completing his first compositions while a young boy. He entered law school for a while, but decided that he would rather become a professional pianist. Moving into the household of Friedrich Wiech to study piano with him, Schumann gradually became more interested in composition. This was because his right hand became permanently injured due to his using wooden splints to improve his fingering technique.

Schumann eventually realized his love for Clara Wieck, the daughter of Friedrich. Schumann's courtship and eventual marriage to the highly talented concert pianist is one of the most famous romances in music. Clara sacrificed her own career to marry Robert in 1840, raising their children and encouraging Schumann's ambitions as a composer.

Besides his interest in piano performance and composition, Schumann also showed great promise in music journalism, for he founded the *Neue Zeitschrift für Music* in 1834 to promote what he thought was important music for his time. Additionally, he formed an intimate group of his friends into the *Davidsbüdler* to support all that was new and imaginative in the arts

With a number of important piano pieces already completed, 1840 was also the year that Robert Schumann turned exclusively to composing songs. He wrote some of his finest lieder in that year, including groups of songs and a series of cycles titled *Myrthen* (Myrtles), *Dicherliebe* (A Poet's Love) and *Frauenliebe und Leben* (A Woman's Love and Life). Working as both a pianist and composer, Schumann made the piano share in the emotion of such songs, often giving the final musical statement of a piece to the piano.

Schumann's *Myrthen*, Op. 25, was his wedding gift to Clara. This cycle of 26 songs was titled "Myrtles" after the blossom traditionally associated with marriage festivities. Drawn from the works of esteemed German poets, the theme of this cycle is that of conjugal love. The words of "*Die Lotosblume,*" the seventh song in *Myrthen*, are from *Buch der Lieder* of 1827, a collection of most of Heinrich Heine's poetry up to that time. This collection also provided the poems for *Dichterliebe*.

Schumann believed that the piano should not merely accompany the voice, but it should communicate with the poetry. For example in the beautiful setting of "*Die Lotosblume,*" the piano begins with repeated chords, which provide a mood of calm and expectancy. The voice then unites with the piano by sounding notes which spell the name Clara (C-G-A-G#-A), a motive which appears numerous times in Schumann's songs. When the left hand joins the right hand in the treble clef, the intensity grows as the flower faces her lover, the Moon, and blooms beautifully. Schumann's diatonic harmonies contrasted with moments of chromaticism possibly suggest that the innocence of love also involves a more sensual feeling.

This nature scene of the lotus flower avoiding the Sun in anticipation of her lover, the Moon, is presented here in the original key of F major. The metronomic indication and additional dynamics have been added to Schumann's original version of this lied.

PRONUNCIATION GUIDE

Die lo-tos-blu-me äng-stigt

di lo-tɔs-blu-mə ɛŋ - stɪçt

sich vor der Son-ne Pracht,

zɪç fɔr der zɔ - nə praxt,

und mit ge-senk-tem Haup-te

ʊnt mɪt gə-zɛŋk-təm haʊp - tə

er-war-tet sie träu-mend die Nacht.

ɛr-var- tət zi: trɔʏ-mənt di naxt.

Der Mond, der ist ihr Buh-le,

der mont, der ɪst i:r bu: - lə

er weckt sie mit sei - nem Licht,

er vɛkt zi: mɪt zaɪ-nəm lɪçt,

und ihm ent-schlei-ert sie freund-lich

ʊnt i:m ɛnt-ʃlaɪ - ərt zi: frɔʏnt - lɪç

ihr from-mes Blu-men-ge-sicht.

i:r frɔ - mes blu:-mən-gə-zɪçt.

Sie blüht und glüht und leuch-tet,

zi: blyt ʊnt glyt   ʊnt lɔʏç - tət,

und star-ret stumm in die Höh';

ʊnt ʃta - rət ʃtʊm   ɪn di hø:;

sie duf-tet und wei-net und zit-tert

zi: duf-tət ʊnt vaɪ-nət ʊnt tsɪ-tərt

vor Lie-be und Lie-bes weh,

fo:r li - bə ʊnt li - bəs ve:,

vor Lie-be und Lie-bes weh.

fo:r li - bə ʊnt li - bəs ve:.

Footnotes to German Pronunciation

• In multiple syllable words, the syllables that should be stressed are underlined.

• [r] should be flipped.

TRANSLATION

The lotus flower is afraid
of the sun's splendor,
and with lowered head
she dreamily awaits the night.

The moon, he is her lover,
he wakes her with his light,
and to him she kindly unveils
her devout flower-face;

she blooms and glows and shines
and stares silently upwards;
she sends out fragrance and weeps and trembles
with love and love's pain.

12. Die Lotosblume
(The Lotus Flower)

German words by **HEINRICH HEINE** (1797–1856)
English words by **PATRICK M. LIEBERGEN**

Op. 25, No. 7
Music by **ROBERT SCHUMANN** (1810–1856)
Edited by **PATRICK M. LIEBERGEN**

*Ziemlich langsam: Rather slowly

10

Mond, der ist___ ihr Buh - le, er weckt sie mit sei - nem
moon, who is___ her lov - er, a - wakes her with ra - diant

13

Licht, und ihm ent - schlei - ert sie freund - lich ihr
light, the flower in all of her beau - ty un -

16

from - mes Blu - men - ge - sicht. Sie blüht und glüht und
veils___ her face through the night. She blooms and glows und

18 *poco a poco accel.*

19

leuch - tet, und star - ret stumm in die Höh';___ sie
splen - dour, and gaz - es up to the sky,___ her

duf - tet und wei - net und zit - tert vor Lie - be und Lie - bes
pe - tals now fra - grant and weep - ing send love to the moon___ on

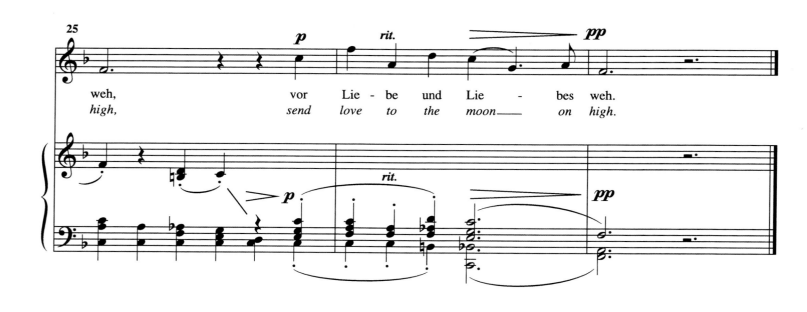

weh, vor Lie - be und Lie - bes weh.
high, send love to the moon___ on high.

O Rest in the Lord

Felix Mendelssohn (1809–1847)

In his brief life of only thirty-eight years, Felix Mendelssohn composed a great amount of music in most of the instrumental and vocal forms of his time. Born into a privileged family in Hamburg, Germany, he had many excellent experiences as a performer, composer and conductor at a very early age. During his lifetime, Mendelssohn traveled widely to many countries for his composing and conducting assignments. He went to England ten times and was once entertained at Buckingham Palace by Queen Victoria.

Mendelssohn's training in the music of Bach, Handel, and Mozart greatly contributed to his development as a composer. In fact, Mendelssohn is credited with revitalizing the music of Johann Sebastian Bach. When he conducted Bach's *St. Matthew Passion* in 1829, it was the first performance of that work since Bach's death seventy-nine years before. Mendelssohn's knowledge of the techniques and materials of past masters is evident in much of his creative output, particularly in his choral works.

Mendelssohn's choral works are among his greatest achievements as a composer. His oratorios, particularly *St. Paul* and *Elijah*, are highly regarded for their great appeal to performers and audiences alike. Composed for four soloists, an S.A.T.B. choir with incidental solo singers, and orchestra, *Elijah* was first conducted by Mendelssohn in 1846 for the Birmingham Festival in England. Originally written in German, the oratorio is usually heard today in Mendelssohn's English version. It is based upon the Old Testament story (I Kings 17) of Elijah, a prophet who predicts three years of drought because the children of Israel have turned away from God ("Yahweh").

"O Rest in the Lord" appears in the second part of the oratorio in response to Elijah's discouragement. After Elijah becomes very low in spirit and asks for death, an angel brings comfort to him with this aria. One of the best known solos from *Elijah*, "O Rest in the Lord" is normally performed by an alto in the presentation of this large-scale work. In this edition, this solo has been transposed up a minor third from the original.

The keyboard accompaniment of "O Rest in the Lord" is a reduction of the original instrumental parts. The editor has also contributed tempo and dynamic indications.

13. O Rest in the Lord

Psalm 37

from ELIJAH
Music by **FELIX MENDELSSOHN** (1809–1847)
Edited and arranged by **PATRICK M. LIEBERGEN**

Expressively and smoothly (♩ = ca. 56)

O rest in the Lord, wait pa-tient-ly for Him, and He shall give thee thy heart's de - sires: O rest in the Lord, wait pa-tient-ly for Him, and He shall give thee thy heart's de - sires, and He shall

O Come, O Come, Emmanuel

(Veni, veni, Emanuel)
15th c. French melody

Adapted by Thomas Helmore (1811–1890)

"O Come, O Come, Emmanuel" is an arrangement of a very famous Advent carol. The original Latin words are based on a series of antiphons which were first sung in the medieval Catholic church during the week of vesper services prior to Christmas Eve. These brief statements were originally seven in number. However, a number of additional verses have been added since then. The first translation of the Latin words into English was by John Mason Neale in 1851, who revised it in 1853.

The chant-like melody is also of medieval origins and was first published with Neale's translation in the second part of Thomas Helmore's *Hymnal Noted* in 1854. Recent research indicates that the melody was probably first sung in France.

This arrangement of the well-known tune provides two of the original antiphon texts in Latin along with a new keyboard accompaniment and optional flute part. The work should be performed very legato, and each phrase should receive a subtle crescendo and decrescendo, without a feeling of meter, to enhance the natural ebb and flow. Additionally, the singer should gently energize the normally stressed syllables of either the English or Latin words.

This arrangement of "O Come, O Come, Emmanuel" is excerpted and adapted from *The Christmas Light: A Masterwork Cantata for Advent or Christmas* (published by Alfred Music, No. 4947), edited and arranged by Patrick M. Liebergen for S.A.T.B. chorus, keyboard, soloists and narrator with optional children's chorus. A separate S.A.T.B. version is also available (published by Alfred Music, No. 11427).

PRONUNCIATION GUIDE

Ve-ni, ve-ni, E-ma-nu-el,
ve̱-ni, ve̱-ni ɛ-ma̱-nu-ɛl,

Cap-ti-vum sol-ve Is-ra-el,
kɑp-ti̱-vum so̱l-vɛ is̱-ɾɑ-ɛl,

Qui ge - mit in ex-i-li-o
kwi dʒɛ̱-mit in ɛ-ksi̱-li-ɔ

Pri-va-tus De-i Fi-li-o.
pɾi-vɑ̱-tus de̱-i fi̱-li-ɔ.

Gau-de! Gau-de! E-ma-nu-el
gɑːu-dɛ! gɑ̱ːu-dɛ! ɛ-ma̱-nu-ɛl

Na-sce-tur pro te, Is-ra-el.
nɑ-ʃɛ̱ - tuɾ pɾɔ tɛ, is̱-ɾɑ-ɛl.

Ve-ni, O Jes-se Vir-gu-la,
ve̱-ni, ɔ je̱ - sɛ viɾ̱-gu-lɑ,

Ex hos-tis tu-os un-gu-la;
ɛks ɔ̱s - tis tu̱-ɔs uṉ-gu-lɑ;

De spe-cu tu-os tar-ta-ri,
dɛ spe̱-ku tu̱-ɔs tɑɾ̱-tɑ-ɾi,

E-duc, et an-tro ba-ra-thri.
ɛ̱-duk, ɛt aṉ-tɾɔ ba̱-ɾɑ-tɾi.

Gau-de! Gau-de! E-ma-nu-el
gɑ̱ːu-dɛ! gɑ̱ːu-dɛ! ɛ-ma̱-nu-ɛl

Na-sce-tur pro te, Is-ra-el.
nɑ-ʃɛ̱-tuɾ pɾɔ tɛ, is̱-ɾɑ-ɛl.

Ve-ni, ve-ni, E-ma-nu-el, Ve-ni.
ve̱ ni, ve̱-ni ɛ-ma̱-nu-ɛl, ve̱-ni.

Footnotes to Latin Prounciation

• In multiple syllable words, the syllables that should be stressed are underlined.

• [ɾ] should be flipped.

14. O Come, O Come, Emmanuel

(Veni, veni, Emanuel)

VENI, VENI EMANUEL, 9th c.
Translated by
JOHN M. NEALE (1818–1866)

15th c. French melody
Adapted by **THOMAS HELMORE** (1811–1890)
Edited and arranged by **PATRICK M. LIEBERGEN**

O come, O come Em-man-u-el,
And ran-som cap-tive Is-ra-el,
That mourns in lone-ly ex-ile

Ve-ni, ve-ni, E-ma-nu-el,
Cap-ti-vum sol-ve Is-ra-el,
Qui ge-mit in ex-i-li

*Optional flute part is on page 192.
** Optional—right hand tacet m. 1–4 if flute plays.

* Optional—right hand tacet m. 17–20 if flute plays.

O come, Thou Day-spring, come_____ and cheer Our spir-its by your ad - vent here; Dis - perse the gloom-y clouds_____ of night, And death's dark shad-ows put_____ to flight. Re -

Ve - ni, O Jes - se Vir - gu - la, Ex hos-tis tu-os un - gu - la; spe - cu tu - os tar - ta - ri, duc, et an-tro ba - ra - thri. Gau -

*Optional—right hand tacet to end if flute plays.

O Holy Night
(Cantique de Noël)

Adolphe Adam (1803–1856)

"O Holy Night" is one of the most beloved Christmas solos ever written. The original French words were written by Placide Cappeau in the middle of the nineteenth century. Cappeau was both a wine dealer and the mayor of the small French town called Roquemaure. Upon a request from his parish priest to write a poem for Chistmas Mass, Cappeau completed the words and then turned to one of his friends, Adolphe Adam, for a musical setting. Although Adam was of Jewish ancestry, his friendship with Cappeau moved Adam to complete an original score to Cappeau's words.

Adolphe Adam was a very successful composer in France during his lifetime, with over eighty stage works to his credit. Born in Paris, he decided at an early age to compose for the theatre. He first studied piano with his father Jean-Louis Adam, who was a piano teacher at the Paris Conservatory. After further study in organ and composition, he composed for vaudeville theatres and later achieved moderate success in composition contests. Eventually, Adam devoted most of his time to composing operas and ballets.

Adam was an important contributor to nineteenth century French opera, and his *Le Chalet* was an especially popular opera. Despite the popularity of his comic operas, Adam preferred to write ballets. *Giselle* was his most successful ballet and is still performed today. This prolific composer also produced piano arrangements, transcriptions of favorite arias, many light songs and ballads, masses, motets, and choruses for male voices. Toward the end of his career, Adam became an opera house proprietor, a music critic, and a professor of composition at the Paris Conservatory. "O Holy Night" is his only well-known vocal work.

This solo became quite popular in France when it was introduced with the original French words. However, "O Holy Night" was brought to a whole new audience in America in the nineteenth century through the English version of John Sullivan Dwight. A gifted writer and founder of *Dwight's Journal of Music*, this retired Unitarian minister translated the original French lyrics into English and published it in his magazine and several songbooks. The song quickly became one of the most popular Christmas songs in America.

This edition includes the addition of tempo and dynamic indications, and the editor has transposed the original publication of Alexander Grus up a half step for high voice.

The grace notes which are found in measures 10, 22, 40, 52, 70 and 82 should be sung quickly and on the beat. Given the song's lengthy duration, the singer may wish to perform only one or two verses as circumstances dictate.

PRONUNCIATION GUIDE

1.

Mi-nuit, Chré-tiens, c'est l'heu-re so-len-nel-le
mi-nɥi, kʀe-t̯jɛ̃ se lœ - ʀə so-la-nɛ-lə

Où l'Hom-me Dieu des-cen-dit jus-qu'à nous,
u lɔ - mə djø de-ʃɑ̃ - di ʒy-skɑ nu,

Pour ef-fa-cer la tache o -ri-gi-nel-le,
puʀ e-fa-se la tɑ ʃo-ʀi-ʒi-nɛ-lə,

Et de son Père ar-rê-ter le cour-roux.
e də sõ pɛ ʀɑ-ʀɛ-te lə ku - ʀu.

Le mon-de‿en-tier tres-sail-le d'es-pé-ran-ce
lə mõ - dɑ̃-t̯je tʀɛ-sɑ - je dɛ - spe-ʀɑ̃-sə

A cet-te nuit qui lui donne un Sau-veur!
ɑ sɛ-tə nɥi ki lyi dɔ nœ so - vœʀ!

Peu-ple‿à ge-noux! At-tends ta dé-li-vran-ce!
pœ-plɑ ʒə-nu! a-tɑ̃ ta de-li-vʀɑ̃ - sə!

No-ël! No-ël! voi - ci le Ré-demp-teur!
nɔ-ɛl! nɔ-ɛl! vwa-si lə ʀe-dɑ̃ - tœʀ!

No-ël! No-ël! voi - ci le Ré-demp-teur!
nɔ-ɛl! nɔ-ɛl! vwa-si lə ʀe-dɑ̃ - tœʀ!

2.

De no-tre foi   que la lu-mière ar-den-te
də no-trə fwa kə la ly-mjɛ rar dɑ̃ - tə

nous gui-de tous au ber-ceau de l'en-fant,
nu   gi - də tu   zo bɛr-so   də lɑ̃ - fɑ̃,

comme au-tre-fois une é - toi - le bril-lan-te
kɔ   mo-trə-fwa zy ne-twa-lə bri - jɑ̃ - tə

y con-dui-sit les chefs de l'O-ri-ent.
i kɔ̃ - dɥɪ-zi le ʃɛf   də lo - ri-ɑ̃.

Le Roi des rois naît dans une hum-ble crè-che;
lə rwa de rwa ne dɑ̃   zy nœ̃ - blə krɛ-ʃə;

puis-sants du jour, fiers de vo-tre gran-deur,
pɥi - sɑ̃   dy ʒur, fjɛr də vɔ-trə grɑ̃ - dœr,

à vo-tre_or-gueil c'est de là qu'un Dieu prê-che;
a vɔ-trɔr - gœj se   də la kœ̃   djø   prɛ-ʃə;

cour-bez vos fronts de-vant le Ré-demp-teur,
kur - be vo frɔ̃   də-vɑ̃ lə re-dɑ̃ - tœr,

cour-bez vos fronts de-vant le Ré-demp-teur.
kur - be vo frɔ̃   də-vɑ̃ lə re-dɑ̃ - tœr.

3.

Le Ré-demp-teur a bri-sé toute en-tra-ve,
lə re-dɑ̃ - tœr a bri-ze tu   tɑ̃-tra-və,

La terre est li-bre_et le ciel est ou-vert;
la tɛ-re li-bre lə sjel ɛ tu-vɛr;

Il voit un frè-re_où n'é-tait qu'un es-cla-ve,
il vwa tœ̃ frɛ ru   ne-te kœ̃   nɛ-sklɑ-və,

L'a-mour u-nit ceux qu-en-chaî-nait le fer.
la - mur y-ni sø   kɑ̃ - ʃɛ - ne lə fɛr.

Qui lui di-ra no-tre re-con-nais-san-ce?
ki   lɥi di-ra nɔ-trə rə-kɔ-nɛ - sɑ̃ - sə?

C'est pour nous tous qu'il naît, qu'il souf-fre_et meurt.
se   pur nu tus kil ne kil su - fre   mœr.

Peu-ple, de-bout, Chan-te ta dé-li-vran-ce,
pœ - plə də-bu, ʃɑ̃ - tə ta de-li-vrɑ̃ - sə,

No-ël! No-ël! chan-tons le Ré-demp-teur.
nɔ-ɛl! nɔ-ɛl! ʃa - tɔ̃ lə re-dɑ̃ - tœr.

No-ël! No-ël! chan-tons le Ré-demp-teur.
nɔ-ɛl! nɔ-ɛl! ʃa - tɔ̃ lə re-dɑ̃ - tœr.

Footnote to French Pronunciation

• In multiple syllable words, the syllables that should be stressed are underlined.

• [r] should be flipped.

• [˜] indicates that the vowel below it should be nasalized.

15. O Holy Night
(Cantique de Noël)

Words of **PLACIDE CAPPEAU** (1808–1877)
Translated by **JOHN S. DWIGHT** (1813–1893)

Music by **ADOLPHE ADAM** (1803–1856)
Edited and arranged by **PATRICK M. LIEBERGEN**

night____ when Christ was born! ____ O night____ di-
ci____ le Ré - demp - teur! ____ No - ël! ____ No-

vine, _____ O night, O____ night di - vine!
ël! _____ voi - ci le____ Ré - demp - teur!

Led by the light____ of Faith se - rene - ly
De no - tre foi____ que la lu - mière ar-

Panis angelicus
(O Lord, I Pray to Thee)

César Franck (1822–1890)

Born in Liege, Belgium, César Franck was already an accomplished pianist by the age of eleven. After early musical training in Belgium, he entered the Paris Conservatory in 1837. Franck left the conservatory in 1842 to teach and compose on a more regular basis.

A renowned composer, teacher and organist in Paris, Franck was one of the most important French musicians during the second half of the nineteenth century. He was the founder of the French School, which was known for its polyphonic compositional style, and he had a profound influence upon his students.

In 1858, Franck was made organist at the church of St. Clotilde in Paris, succeeding Théodore Dubois in that post. Especially revered for his improvisation, Franck played the magnificent organ in that church until his death. He worked on his oratorio *Les Beatitudes* for over ten years and produced some of his best music in the latter portion of his life, including Sonata for Piano and Violin, Symphony in D minor, String Quartet in D Major and Three Chorales for Organ.

Franck is especially revered today for his symphonic, chamber, and keyboard works. His art songs, oratorios, masses, and other smaller vocal works have remained little known. However, his *"Panis angelicus"* is widely performed by soloists and choirs alike. Written for performance at the church of St. Clotilde, it was probably based on an improvisation which Franck played during a Christmas service in 1861. The original Latin text is the sixth verse of the Corpus Christi hymn *Sacris solemnis*. Composed as a singular work, Franck latter integrated it into his *Messe à 3 voix*.

The original version of *"Panis angelicus"* was for tenor soloist and an accompaniment of organ, harp, cello, and double-bass. The work is presented here in its original key for voice, flute (or C instrument) or cello (please see pages 194 and 195 for flute and cello parts). As provided in Franck's original score, the cello part in this publication first presents the melody as a prelude to the opening vocal entrance. The flute part is a duplication of the cello part, written two octaves higher. The keyboard part provided in this arrangement is a reduction of all the instrumental parts provided in Franck's score.

Dynamic and tempo indications and English words have been added to this edition. This beautiful song should be performed very legato while energizing the normally stressed syllables of the Latin or English words.

PRONUNCIATION GUIDE

Pa-nis an-ge-li-cus, fit pa-nis ho-mi-num,
pɑ-nis ɑn-ʤɛ-li-kus, fit pɑ-nis ɔ - mi-num,

Dat pa-nis coe-li-cus fi-gu-ris ter-mi-num.
dɑt pɑ-nis ʧɛ-li-kus fi-ɡu-ris tɛɾ-mi-num.

O res mi-ra-bi-lis man-du-cat Do-mi-num,
ɔ ɾɛs mi-ɾɑ-bi-lis mɑn-du-kɑt dɔ-mi-num,

Pau-per, pau-per, ser-vus, et hu-mi-lis,
pɑːu-pɛɾ, pɑːu-pɛɾ, sɛɾ-vus, ɛt u - mi-lis,

Pau-per, pau-per, ser-vus, et hu-mi-lis.
pɑːu-pɛɾ, pɑːu-pɛɾ, sɛɾ-vus, ɛt u - mi-lis.

TRANSLATION

The bread of the angels becomes the bread of humankind,
This heavenly bread gives an end to all earthly forms.
O marvelous thing, nourished on the Lord
are a poor man, a servant and a humble one.

Footnotes to Latin Pronunciation

• In multiple syllable words, the syllables that should be stressed are capitalized.

• [ɾ] should be flipped.

16. Panis angelicus
(O Lord, I Pray to Thee)
With optional flute and cello

English words by
PATRICK M. LIEBERGEN

from *Messe à voix*
Music by **CÉSAR FRANCK** (1822–1890)
Edited and arranged by **PATRICK M. LIEBERGEN**

Optional flute and cello parts are on pages 194 and 195, respectively.

My Lovely Celia

George Monro (1680–1731)

Performed in many concert halls since the early twentieth century, "My Lovely Celia" is the combined work of two English composers, George Monro and Henry James Lane Wilson.

The melody was written by the little known English Composer George Monro, whose last name is also spelled Monroe and Munro. He was an organist at St. Peter's Cornhill and played harpsichord in the orchestra of Goodman Fields Theatre from 1729 until his death in London in 1731. Monro wrote music for Henry Fielding's comedy *The Temple Beau* and numerous songs, including the popular "My Lovely Celia."

It was Henry James Lane Wilson who wrote the accompaniment to this tune and had it published in his collection of 1899 titled *Old English Melodies*. In his arrangement, Wilson used only two of Monro's three verses and slightly altered the words.

Wilson was a prolific writer of songs, including his cycles *Dorothy's Wedding Day* and *Flora's Holiday*, and a highly talented arranger of old English melodies. Born in Gloucester in 1871, he became quite active as a musician in London. Wilson composed music, played keyboards, performed as a soloist and accompanied some of the most famous singers of his day on recital tours.

Wilson's accompaniment to Monro's melody is featured here with the addition of metronic and dynamic indications. Strophic and set to a sentimental text of unknown authorship, this flowing song has been transposed a major second lower than the original key of G major.

17. My Lovely Celia

Words of unknown authorship

Music by **GEORGE MONRO** (1680–1731)
Based on the arrangement of **HENRY JAMES LANE WILSON** (1899–1915)
Edited by **PATRICK M. LIEBERGEN**

* This breath mark is in Wilson's original arrangement.

melt - ing— beams so oft— a - rise; My

heart's— en - chant - ed with— thy— charms, O

take— me, dy - ing, to— your arms.—

I Will Sing New Songs

Antonín Dvořák (1841–1904)

Antonín Dvořák was a renowned Czech composer. Born near Prague in Muhlhausen, Bohemia, he studied piano, organ, violin and singing as a child. He was a violist in the National Theatre of Prague and a church organist for a number of years. While his earlier compositions were influenced by the styles of the great European masters such as Beethoven, Schubert, Wagner, and Brahms, Dvořák's later compositions became more nationalistic in style, often incorporating the folk tunes of his homeland.

Dvořák wrote symphonies, operas, symphonic poems, overtures, various works for instrumental solo with orchestra, chamber works (quartets and quintets), oratorios and other choral works, and songs. His best known work is the Symphony in E Minor, also known as *From the New World*. It was written in the United States in 1893, a year after Dvořák accepted a position as director of the National Conservatory of Music of America in New York. Suggestive of spirituals and Native American melodies, the work was first performed by the New York Philharmonic Orchestra on December 15, 1893, in Carnegie Hall. Dvořák's other significant works are the overture *Carnival*, Concerto for Cello, *American String Quartet*, the oratorios *Stabat Mater* and *The Specter's Bride*, and many of his songs.

Gypsy Songs (Op. 55) and *Biblical Songs* (Op. 99) are the best known of Dvořák's vocal solos. Shortly after he completed the ten pieces in *Biblical Songs*, he orchestrated the original piano accompaniment of the first five. He completed that orchestration in New York in 1896. But it is unavailable today because Dvořák apparently mislaid the score and was not able to have it published.

Dvořák used the seventeenth century Czech version of the *Kralice Bible* when he referred to the *Book of Psalms* in setting these songs. He later changed notes and rhythms in his original melodies to accommodate German and English texts.

"I Will Sing New Songs," which appears as No. 5 in *Biblical Songs*, is based upon Dvořák's English version. In this edition, the original has been transposed up one whole step. Also, the editor has included a metronome marking and additions to the dynamics. Beautifully written for the voice, this song employs a folk-like melody and rhythm which should be performed vigorously and majestically.

18. I Will Sing New Songs

Words adapted from the Book of Psalms
by **ANTONÍN DVOŘÁK**

Music by **ANTONÍN DVOŘÁK** (1841–1904)
Edited by **PATRICK M. LIEBERGEN**

Ev - 'ry day will I ex - tol Thee, and will bless Thy
ho - ly name, — I will bless Thy ho - ly name.
Great is God and great His mer - cy. Who shall tell of all His great - ness?

Se tu m'ami
(If You Love Me)

Alessandro Parisotti (1853-1913)

Although probably written by Alessandro Parisotti, *"Se tu m'ami"* has been attributed to the Baroque composer Giovanni Battista Pergolesi (1710–1736) since the latter part of the nineteenth century. The song first appeared in Parisotti's first volume of *Arie Antiche*, an anthology of songs from the seventeenth and eighteenth centuries published by Ricordi in Milan, Italy in 1885. Pergolesi is listed as the composer of *"Se tu m'ami"* in this three volume collection. However no early manuscript of this song has ever been found. It is now believed that Parisotti wrote the song because of his great interest in early music. *"Se tu m'ami"* is Parisotti's most famous work.

Parisotti was born in Rome and lived there his entire life. He became the secretary of the Accademia di Santa Cecilia in 1880 and distinguished himself as a musicologist, researching and editing numerous songs from the Baroque period. Parisotti provided piano realizations of the original figured bass parts of those songs and carefully completed new editions by consulting original sources. His efforts were ultimately published in his *Arie Antiche*, a revival of forgotten songs that would eventually be used for teaching vocal technique and for the concert stage.

Parisotti set *"Se tu m'ami"* to the words of the Italian poet Paolo Antonio Rolli, a librettist for both Handel and Bononcini, who lived in London. The original Italian words of this song are found in *Di canzonette e di cantate libri due*, published by T. Edlin in London in 1727.

Parisotti attempted to make *"Se tu m'ami"* look like it was written by a Baroque composer by selecting a poem from the early eighteenth century. However, the work should be performed in the style of the late nineteenth century. Parisotti actually provided quite a romantic feeling, with numerous dynamic and tempo changes that are not typical of Baroque music. Originally published in *Arie Antiche* in F minor, the editor has modernized the original nineteenth century notation for today's performer.

PRONUNCIATION GUIDE

Se tu m'a-mi, se tu so-spi-ri
sɛ tu mɑ - <u>mi</u>, sɛ tu sɔ-<u>spi</u>-ɾi

sol per me, gen - til pa-stor,
sɔl per me, dʒɛn-<u>til</u> pɑ-<u>stor</u>,

ho do-lor dei tuoi mar-ti-ri,
ɔ dɔ-<u>lor</u> dei twɔi mɑr-<u>ti</u>-ɾi,

ho di-let-to del tuo‿a-mor.
ɔ di-<u>lɛt</u>:to del tuɔɑ - <u>mor</u>.

Ma se pen-si che so-let-to
mɑ sɛ <u>pɛn</u>-si kɛ sɔ-<u>lɛt</u>:tɔ

io ti deb-ba ri-a-mar,
iɔ ti <u>dɛb</u>:bɑ <u>ri</u>-ɑ-mɑr,

pa-sto-rel-lo, sei sog-get-to
pɑ-stɔ-<u>rɛl</u>:lo, sɛi sɔd:<u>dʒɛt</u>:tɔ

fa-cil -men-te‿a t'in gan-nar.
fɑ-tʃil-<u>men</u>-tɛɑ tiŋ gɑn:<u>nɑr</u>.

Bel-la ro-sa por-po-ri-na
<u>bɛl</u>:lɑ <u>rɔ</u>-zɑ pɔr-pɔ-<u>ri</u>-nɑ

og-gi Sil-via sceg-lie - rà,
<u>ɔd</u>:dʒi <u>sil</u>-vjɑ ʃɛʎ:ʎɛ - <u>rɑ</u>,

con la scu-sa del-la spi-na
kɔn lɑ <u>sku</u>-zɑ <u>del</u>:lɑ <u>spi</u>-nɑ

do-man poi la sprez-ze-rà.
<u>do</u>-mɑn pɔi lɑ sprɛt:tsɛ-<u>rɑ</u>.

Ma de-gli‿uo-mi-ni‿il con-si-glio
mɑ dɛ-<u>ʎiwɔ</u> - mi-<u>nil</u> kɔn-<u>si</u>-ʎɔ

io per me non se-gui-rò.
iɔ pɛr me nɔn sɛ-gwi-<u>rɔ</u>.

Non per-chè mi pia-ce‿il gi - glio
non pɛr-<u>ke</u> mi <u>pjɑ</u>-tʃɛil <u>dʒi</u>-ʎɔ

gli‿al-tri fio-ri sprez-ze-rò.
ʎiɑl - tri <u>fjɔ</u>-ɾi <u>sprɛt</u>:sɛ-ɾɔ.

Footnotes to Italian Pronunciation

• In multiple syllable words, the syllables that should be stressed are underlined.

• [ɾ] should be flipped.

• [r] should be trilled.

• [ʎ] indicates a similar sound to [lj] in the word "million"—[mɪ-ljən], requiring only one tongue action, as in the word "giglio"—[dʒi-ʎɔ].

• Certain double consonants can be sustained on a pitch while maintaining a legato line, such as those in the words "pastorello" and "gannar." The singer should take time for the singable double consonants in each of these words from the preceding musical note.

• There are other double consonants, such as those in the words "diletto" and "debba," which interrupt the legato line when pronounced correctly. For example, when singing the word "diletto" [di-lɛt:tɔ], the singer should briefly stop on the first [t], creating a slight silence before the sounding of the second [t].

TRANSLATION

If you love me, if you sigh
only for me, kind shepherd,
I am sorry for your suffering,
I delight in your love.
But if you think that I
should only love you in return,
little shepherd,
you are easily deceived.

Today Silvia will choose
a beautiful purple rose,
Tomorrow, then, she will despise it
because of its thorn.
But I will not follow
the advice of men.
I will not despise the other flowers
just because the lily pleases me.

19. Se tu m'ami

(If You Love Me)

Italian words by
PAOLO ANTONIO ROLLI (1687–1765)
English words by **PATRICK M. LIEBERGEN**

Music by **ALESSANDRO PARISOTTI** (1853–1913)
Edited by **PATRICK M. LIEBERGEN**

Se tu m'a - mi, se tu so - spi - ri sol per
If you love me, if you sigh loud - ly on - ly

me, gen - til pa - stor, ho do - lor dei tuoi mar - ti - ri,
for me, kind shep - herd, I am sor - rowed in your suf - f'ring,

Bel - la ro - sa por - po - ri - na og - gi Sil - via sceg - lie - rà,
Soon the red rose will be chos - en, picked by Sil - via to hold near,

con la scu - sa del - la spi - na do - man poi la sprez - ze - rà,
She will scorn it when she feels the thorn that pricks her with - out fear,

do - man poi la sprez - ze - rà. Ma de - gli uo - mi - ni il con - si - glio
thorn that pricks her with - out fear. I'll not ev - er lis - ten to the

io per me non se - gui - rò. Non per - chè mi pia - ce il gi - glio
men who tell me what to do. Ev - en though I like the li - lies,

The Virgin's Slumber Song
(Mariä Wiegenlied)

Max Reger (1873–1916)

A highly talented composer, keyboardist, conductor and teacher, Max Reger was one of the greatest and most widely performed composers at the beginning of the twentieth century. Born in Brand, Bavaria, he prepared for a music career by studying piano, organ, theory and other subjects at various music schools in Germany. He then held a variety of positions in Wiesbaden, Munich, Leipzig and Meininger while composing. His final teaching position was at the University of Leipzig as the Director of Music from 1907 until his death.

Reger conducted many of his works in Europe, England, and Russia during his tenure at Leipzig. He became widely respected for his skillful polyphonic writing in the style of early masters, his use of complicated harmonies and his unwavering interest in the absolute forms of the Classic and Romantic periods. Reger especially admired the contrapuntal technique of Johann Sebastian Bach. Fugues, canons and non-imitative forms of counterpoint are numerous in his works.

He composed in all of the forms of his time except opera and his compositional output of 146 opus numbers and numerous works without opus numbers was tremendous for his brief life. Reger also wrote extensively for the voice, completing choral compositions and solo lieder.

Some of his most attractive pieces were written on a small scale, such as "The Virgin's Slumber Song." Completed in 1904, he included it in a set of sixty lieder titled *Schlichte Weisen*, Op. 76. Reger wrote "The Virgin's Slumber Song" by transforming the opening phrase of the folk-like melody known as "Joseph Dearest, Joseph, Mild" (or *"Resonet In Laudibus"*) into an art song. His setting is complemented with an accompaniment which seems to be a reduction of an orchestral score, although it is not. The orchestral song was popular in the twentieth century, and Reger often arranged lieder of the Romantic composers as orchestral songs for use in his own concerts. The lovely melody and accompaniment of this song suggest the rocking of a cradle.

Reger's original has been transposed up a major third. Included in this edition are English words by Edward Teschemacher, a lyricist from nineteenth century England with over 1000 songs to his credit. Teschemacher's words for this song are quite singable and have been featured on many popular recordings, although they are not an exact translation of the original German.

PRONUNCIATION GUIDE

Ma-ri-a sitzt am Ro-sen-hag
ma-ṟi-ɑ zɪtst ɑm ṟoː-zən-hɑk

und wiegt ihr Je-sus-kind,
ʊnt vikt iːr jẹ-sus-kɪnt,

durch die Blät-ter lei-se
dʊrç di blẹ - tər lạɪ-zə

weht der war-me Som-mer-wind.
veːt der vạɾ-mə zọ - mər-vɪnt.

Zu ihr-en Fü-ssen
tsuː iː - rən fỵ - sən

singt ein bun-tes Vö-ge-lein:
zɪŋt ɑɪn bụn-təs fọ̈ - gə-lɑɪn:

Schlaf', Kind-lein, sü-sse, schlaf' nun ein!
ʃlɑːf,   kɪnt - lɑɪn, zỵ-sə, ʃlɑf   nun ɑɪn!

Hold ist dein Lä-cheln,
hɔlt   ɪst dɑɪn lẹ-çɛln,

hol-der dei-nes Schlum-mers Lust,
hɔ̣l-dər dạɪ-nəs ʃlụ - mərs lʊst,

leg dein mü-des Köpf-chen
lek dɑɪn mỵ-dəs kœ̣pf-çən

fest an dei-ner Mut-ter Brust!
fest ɑn dạɪ-nər mụ - tər brʊst!

Schlaf', Kind-lein, sü-sse, schlaf' nun ein!
ʃlɑf,   kɪnt - lɑɪn, zỵ-sə, ʃlɑf   nun ɑɪn!

Schlaf', Kind-lein, sü-sse, schlaf' nun ein!
ʃlɑf,   kɪnt - lɑɪn, zỵ-sə, ʃlɑf   nun ɑɪn!

Footnotes to German Pronunciation

• In multiple syllable words, the syllables that should be stressed are underlined.

• [ɾ] should be flipped.

TRANSLATION

Mary sits by the rosebush and rocks her child, Jesus,
the warm summer wind gently blows through the leaves.
A colorful little bird sings at her feet:
Sleep, little child, sweet one, sleep now!

Charming is your smile, lovelier your slumbers delight,
put your weary little head firmly on your mother's breast!
Sleep, little child, sweet one, sleep now!
Sleep, little child, sweet one, sleep now!

20. The Virgin's Slumber Song
(Mariä Wiegenlied)

English words by
EDWARD TESCHEMACHER (1876–1940)
German words by
MARTIN BOELITZ (1874–1921)

Op. 76, No. 52
Music by **MAX REGER** (1873–1916)
Edited by **PATRICK M. LIEBERGEN**

The Call

Ralph Vaughan Williams (1872–1958)

Ralph Vaughan Williams was a great composer and a successful teacher, writer and conductor who revived twentieth century British music. A contributor to nearly all genres, including stage and film music, he developed his unique English style of composition by drawing on the modality of folk song literature and the works of past and early twentieth century composers.

Educated at a young age in theory, piano and violin, he studied at Charterhouse, the Royal College of Music, and Trinity College, Cambridge. He then became a composition student of Charles Stanford and developed a life-long friendship with Gustav Holst, with whom he shared a great interest in the English music of the sixteenth and seventeenth centuries and English folk songs. He joined the Folk Song Society in 1904, collecting, studying and eventually arranging folksongs for modern performance and in his own original compositions. Also in 1904, he became the editor of a new hymnbook which was published in 1906, *The English Hymnal*.

He spent most of his time as a young man studying and composing. He became a student of Max Bruch and Maurice Ravel, eventually serving in World War I and teaching at the Royal College of Music. His private income from his numerous compositional successes enabled Vaughan Williams to research numerous English folk song melodies. A recipient of many honors and awards, including the Gold Medal of the Royal Philharmonic Society of London and the Order of Merit from King George V, Vaughan Williams continued to compose to the end of his life.

Vaughan Williams first composed a number of secular songs before turning to spiritual texts in his setting of vocal solos and choral works. He was particularly drawn to religious words which could have a place in worship and which were often mystical, although he was known to be an agnostic.

"The Call" is the fourth of the five movements of his *Five Mystical Songs* for baritone, chorus and orchestra. Commissioned for the Worcester Three Choirs Festival of 1911, it was first performed in Worcester Cathedral with soloist Campbell McInnes, Festival Chorus and London Symphony Orchestra conducted by Vaughan Williams. Vaughan Williams broke away from the traditional use of only voice and piano by employing the "optional" use of chorus in the first three movements to subtly underscore the soloist with words and vowel sounds. The fourth movement, "The Call," was scored for voice and orchestra alone. Vaughan Williams set the fifth movement for choir and orchestra; however, he provided another version of that movement for voice and orchestra without the choir.

The words of *Five Mystical Songs* are the work of George Herbert (1593-1633), a seventeenth century poet and musician who served as a Public Orator at Cambridge and whose words were set to a number of hymns, such as "Let All the World in Every Corner Sing."

"The Call" is a beautiful, hymn-like setting of Herbert's words, in which the modal harmonies and melismatic passages capture the mystical feeling of the piece. The flowing melody and subtle accompaniment follow the meter of the poem, which speaks of the relationship between God and the person.

Originally set in E-flat major, this version in the transposed key of F major is based on the Steiner and Bell publication for soloist and piano alone.

21. The Call

Words by **GEORGE HERBERT** (1593–1633)

from FIVE MYSTICAL SONGS
Music by **RALPH VAUGHAN WILLIAMS** (1872–1958)

Lo, How a Rose E'er Blooming
(Es ist ein Ros entsprungen)

Hugo Distler (1908–1942)

The well known melody *"Es ist ein Ros entsprungen"* has been set over the centuries by many composers for use during Advent and Christmastide. It originated in the fifteenth century in the Trier region of western Germany and was first published in the Catholic hymnal *Alte catholische geistliche Kirchengesänge* in Cologne in 1599. One of the most famous arrangements of this beloved carol can be found in Part VI of *Musae Sioniae* (1609) by Michael Praetorius.

The Christmas rose has been a symbol of the yuletide season in German lands for centuries, inspiring numerous lyrics and songs in its honor. The original German words of this song provide a wonderful imagery of the newborn child (the rose) coming from the "stem of Jesse." Jesse was the father of King David and the patriarch of Christ's genealogy in many medieval sources. In those sources, Jesse was often depicted as a rose plant. The "stem" refers to the Virgin Mary, who will bring forth the Christ child as foretold by the prophet Isaiah. Theodore Baker's translation of the original German words has been included in this arrangement of Hugo Distler's very beautiful setting of *"Es ist ein Ros entsprungen"* ("Lo, How a Rose E'er Blooming.")

Distler was an important German composer in the early part of the twentieth century. He studied at the Leipzig Conservatory and eventually became organist at the Jakobikirche in Lübeck and taught at various schools of music. In 1940 he taught composition and organ at the Berlin Hochschule, and in 1941 he became director of the Berlin Cathedral Choir. The victim of Nazi persecution, he committed suicide in 1942 before completing his ambitious oratorio, *Die Weltalter*.

Distler's output included numerous sacred and secular choral works, of which the largest is the *Choralpassion*, Op. 7 (1932). He also wrote a concerto for harpsichord and strings and words for piano and organ. Extensively trained in church music, Distler showed a great interest in polyphony and in the ideals of the Baroque composer Heinrich Schütz. Schütz's style profoundly influenced Disler's *Weihnachtsgeschichte*, Op. 10, in which the natural declamation of the text is maintained in all four voices by incorporating a polyrhythmic notation.

Completed in 1933, Distler's *"Es ist ein Ros entsprungen,"* Op. 10, is a multi-sectional work that was originally set for a four-part mixed chamber chorus and four soloists without instrumental accompaniment. This arrangement is adapted from the first section of that work, with the vocal solo based upon the soprano's melody and the accompaniment fashioned from the remaining vocal parts. The editor has added dynamic and tempo indications and has transposed the work one half step higher than the original key.

PRONUNCIATION GUIDE

Es ist ein Ros ent-sprun-gen
ɛs ɪst aɪn roz ɛnt-ʃpru - ŋən

aus ei-ner Wur-zel zart,
aʊs aɪ-nər vur - tsəl tsart,

als uns die Al-ten sun-gen:
als uns di al-tən zu - ŋən:

von Jes-se kam die Art
fɔn jɛ - sə kam di art

und hat ein Blüm-lein bracht
unt hat aɪn blym-laɪn braxt

mit-ten im kal-ten Win-ter,
mɪ-tən ɪm kal-tən vɪn-tər,

wohl zu   der hal-ben Nacht.
voːl tsu der hal-bən naxt.

Das Rös-lein, das ich mei-ne,
das røːs-laɪn, das ɪç maɪ-nə,

da-von E-sai-as sagt,
da-fɔn ɛ-zaɪ-as ʒakt,

hat uns ge-bracht al-lei-ne
hat uns gə-braxt a-laɪ-nə

Ma-rie, die rei-ne Magd.
ma-ri, di raɪ-nə makt.

Aus Got-tes ew-gem Rat
aʊs gɔ - təs ev-gəm rat

hat sie ein Kind ge-bo-ren,
hat zi aɪn kɪnt gə-bo-rən,

wohl zu der hal-ben Nacht.
vol   tsu der hal-bən naxt.

Footnotes to German Pronuncation

• In multiple syllable words, the syllables that should be stressed are underlined.

• [ɾ] should be flipped.

22. Lo, How a Rose E'er Blooming
(Es ist ein Ros entsprungen)

English words by
THEODORE BAKER (1851–1934)

from Weihnachtsgeschichte, Op. 10
by **HUGO DISTLER** (1908–1942)
Arranged by **PATRICK M. LIEBERGEN**

Lo, how a rose e'er bloom - ing from ten - der
Es ist ein Ros ent - sprun - gen aus ei - ner

stem hath sprung, of Jes - se's lin - eage
Wur - zel zart, als uns die Al - ten

com - ing, as those of old have sung.
sun - gen: als von Jes - se kam die Art

Sigh No More, Ladies

Roger Quilter (1877–1953)

Roger Quilter was one of the most prolific and highly esteemed English song writers of the early Twentieth Century. Born into a wealthy family, he was educated at Eton College before continuing his musical studies at the Hoch Conservatory in Frankfurt. Quite familiar with the English style, Quilter was greatly influenced at the German conservatory by Iwan Knorr, a renowned Russian professor of composition, and by his acquaintance with the lieder of the masters, such as Schubert and Schumann. He also enjoyed music of some French composers, especially the melodies of Fauré. Returning to England, he achieved early fame as a writer of English songs when Denham Price performed his *Songs of the Sea* at the Crystal Palace in London in 1900. The premiere performances by Gervase Elwes of his *To Julia*, a song cycle for voice and piano and instruments, in 1905 and *Seven Elizabethan Lyrics*, in 1908 further established Quilter's reputation.

Quilter continued to write songs throughout his life, completing more than 100. Many leading vocalists of his time performed his songs, resulting in more requests for him to work in that medium. However, he also wrote choral, instrumental and stage works. For example, he completed incidental music to *Where The Rainbow Ends,* a children's play about fairy tales which was premiered in 1911. He also wrote light orchestral music, including *A Children's Overture* in 1919, a skillful orchestration of nursery rhymes which became very popular. It was included in the first broadcast concert of the BBC in December, 1922.

His radio opera *The Blue Boar,* composed in 1934, and the opera *Julia,* completed in 1936, were not successful. But several pieces from the latter work, for example "Love at the Inn," were extracted and published as separate songs. Quilter also made many arrangements of traditional songs, such as those included in his 1947 publication titled *The Arnold Book of Old Songs*.

Quilter's original songs are characterized by lyrical melodic lines, imaginative accompaniments with interesting textures, many chromatic harmonies and clear textual declamation. Additionally, his songs reveal a high standard in his choice of poetry. Besides works by Shelley, Keats, Blake and many others, William Shakespeare's works are found in 19 of his settings.

"Sigh No More, Ladies" is found in Quilter's *Four Shakespeare Songs,* Third Set. Op. 30, composed between 1926 and 1933 and originally published by Boosey and Hawkes. Like the majority of his songs, it is strophic. The words of this very popular song are from Act 2, scene 3 of Shakespeare's *Much Ado About Nothing.* In measure 29, "mo" is the shortened version of the word "more." In measure 30, "dumps" refers to a state of sadness, and in measure 35, "leavy" is the old English word for "leafy."

23. Sigh No More, Ladies

Words by **WILLIAM SHAKESPEARE** (1564–1616)

Op. 30, No. 4
Music by **ROGER QUILTER**

When I Think Upon the Maidens

Michael Head (1900–1976)

Michael Head was a distinguished English composer, singer and pianist. He attended the Royal Academy of Music from 1919 through 1925, where he studied composition. An active adjudicator and concert pianist, Head became a professor of piano at that school in 1927. He was known in his day for his extensive recital tours, performing his songs in one-man shows. Head also made broadcasts and several recordings of his piano interpretations.

His first works were published in 1917. In all, Head completed approximately 85 songs and a variety of operatic presentations, including *Key Money* (1960) and *Day Return* (1967) for the Intimate Opera Company, and *After The Wedding* (1969) for the Opera Workshop.

Head's songs are more melodically simple and harmonically conservative than his operas, and many are performed in studios and concert halls today. His most popular songs include "The Little Road to Bethlehem" and "When I Think upon the Maidens."

A performance of "When I Think upon the Maidens" requires quite an extroverted presentation, in which the singer explains that he can't decide which one of his loves he prefers the most. Head clearly indicated his intentions for the performance of this song on his original score. On the copy provided by Boosey and Hawkes, the numerous articulations, such as staccato and marcato, and the changes in registers, harmonies, dynamics and tempi underscore the differences in textual ideas. The pianist should begin the song aggressively in the *presto* tempo indicated by Head. Thereafter, both vocalist and pianist should unify as one in a rhythmic and dramatic presentation of the textual message.

24. When I Think Upon the Maidens

Words by **PHILIP ASHBROOKE**

Music by **MICHAEL HEAD** (1900–1976)

Do they scorn me now I wonder, Did they take it as a game?

Flor - a, Ol - ive, And — the oth - ers, How I hat - ed all their broth - ers!

Ah! _____ Fick - le Cu - pid, Fick - le Cu - pid

At the River

Aaron Copland (1900–1990)

Aaron Copland was a tremendously successful and influential American composer of the twentieth century. Born into a family of Russian-Jewish immigrants, he attended many concerts in the New York area and studied composition with Rubin Goldmark at a young age before traveling to Paris to become a student of Nadia Boulanger.

Copland soon developed his own American style. He was influenced by his musical experiences in Paris at the American Conservatory, the neo-classicism of Stravinsky, nationalistic music of the European composers and the popular music of his time. He employed elements of jazz and folk music in a variety of artistic projects, including ballet, opera and film. Achieving great acclaim early in his life with the premiere of his *Symphony for Organ and Orchestra* in Carnegie Hall, it was in the late 1930s and early 1940s that he became especially well known for his use of American themes in his ballets, such as *Billy the Kid, Rodeo* and *Appalachian Spring*. In his *Appalachian Spring*, he conveyed the spirit of a pioneering community in the Appalachian mountains with his use of the hymn tune "Simple Gifts."

At the same time, Copland wrote orchestral music and music for films, completing *Of Mice and Men, Our Town, The Red Pony* and the Oscar-winning *The Heiress*. Frequently conducting his own works, he also lectured, taught and wrote. His several books include *What To Listen For In Music* (1939) and *Music and Imagination* (1952). In his latter years his interest in serialism and more abstract compositional techniques resulted in works which were not as well received as his previous works. He promoted contemporary composers and organized musical events through much of his career, ceasing to compose works in the 1970's.

Highly revered internationally with memberships and fellowships, Copland's numerous honors in America included honorary doctorates, a Presidential Medal of Freedom, a Kennedy Center Honor, a Medal of the Arts, a Congressional Gold Medal and a Pulitzer Prize.

"At the River" was arranged by Copland in 1952 as part of his *Old American Songs II*, a collection which also includes "Little Horses," "Zion's Wall," "The Golden Willow," and "Ching-a-Ring Chaw." The words and music of "At the River" were written in 1864 by Robert Lowry (1826-1899), a popular Baptist minister and preacher who is best remembered for writing hymn texts and tunes. He served Baptist pastorates in Pennsylvania, New York and New Jersey, was a professor of literature at Bucknell University, became the editor of song collections for Sunday School, and collaborated with many others in writing works for church use.

Lowry's beloved "At the River" was set by Copland in a straightforward arrangement, allowing the simplicity of the words and melody to be clearly heard. Copland provided an accompaniment of mostly block chords with a forward movement of certain motives, most notably the dotted eighth note-sixteenth note rhythmic grouping.

25. At the River
(Hymn Tune)

Adapted by **AARON COPLAND** (1900–1990)

Folk Songs from the United States

Go, Tell It on the Mountain

This tuneful and exuberant spiritual for Christmas is one of the most famous contributions of the African Americans to the vocal repertoire. Although most spirituals in the nineteenth century were songs of sorrow, originally sung to ease the frustration and hopelessness of the enslaved person, a few spirituals were joyful. "Go, Tell It on the Mountain" is unique, for it celebrates the joyful news of Christ's birth.

This spiritual was brought to national prominence after the Civil War through the combined efforts of a family of choral directors and a black choral ensemble. John Wesley Work, an African American choir director at a church in Nashville, Tennessee and a highly talented musician and scholar, first promoted the song in his music ministry and introduced it to members of the Fisk Jubilee Singers, a choral ensemble from a nearby black college. Wesley Work, Jr., then collaborated with his brother Frederick on a new arrangement of "Go, Tell It on the Mountain," giving it a more anthem-like structure for performance by choirs. The Fisk Jubilee Singers began performing their new arrangement in the 1880s in numerous concerts around the country and abroad, further exposing the musical talents of African-Americans. "Go, Tell It on the Mountain" was first published in 1909 in Thomas P. Fenner's book titled *Religious Folk Songs of the Negro as Sung on the Plantations*.

However, it was the son of John Wesley Work Jr. who arranged the version that we know today. John Work III, a graduate of Julliard and scholar of history and music, had his new arrangement published in 1940 in *American Negro Songs and Spirituals*. In recent decades, "Go, Tell It on the Mountain" has remained quite popular for performance in a variety of different genres.

Deep River

"Deep River" is a plea for deliverance out of a life of sorrow and oppression. African-Americans originally sang spirituals to express their need for freedom and a life of peace, in addition to using the songs as a means of communication and a map to the North.

This song includes many biblical allusions typical of other spirituals; for example, the words "deep river" and "Jordan" are used in a metaphor to symbolize the trials of life which must be "crossed" to get to heaven. Certain spiritual leaders in the Bible, such as Moses and Elijah, had to "cross over" with the help of the Lord. The word "Jordan" in this spiritual refers to the river that the Jews had to cross when fleeing Egypt to reach the Promised Land. In America, it was either the Mississippi River or Ohio River that the black slave had to cross to reach freedom in the North.

Another symbolic word is "campground," which to the Negro of the nineteenth century meant a heavenly place. A "campground" was the area in the South where all black and white workers celebrated a bountiful harvest with several joy-filled days of eating and dancing. Additionally, participating in a "gospel feast" was the expectation of the Negro, who believed that earning that heavenly reward would include sitting at the table of the Lord in paradise. The message of this spiritual is that freedom lies in crossing over Jordan, thereby uniting with God in eternal salvation.

Shenandoah

There are many textual variations of this song of the sea, mainly because there is disagreement about the meaning of the word "Shenandoah." Dating from the nineteenth century, one version makes "Shenandoah" an Indian Chief, whose daughter is wooed by an early settler. This very popular version probably originated among the traders traveling the Missouri River. Yet there are other versions with considerable textual differences which only include references to geographical locations. This arrangement includes two of the most popular versions.

Amazing Grace

"Amazing Grace" is one of the best known and popular folk hymns in American history. Published in numerous hymnals and songbooks, it has been recorded by various gospel, folk and popular singing artists, and has also been featured in many arrangements for band, orchestra and choir.

The textual setting of this famous tune is by John Newton. The words refer to his early life and experiences, especially his conversion to Christianity after a life of slave trading and failure. It was after he miraculously survived an eleven hour storm off the coast of Newfoundland in 1748 that he changed his life, becoming a minister and an anti-slavery activist. He eventually authored hymn texts, and he also became a published author of words condemning the slave trade. Newton's "Amazing Grace" is a recollection of his deliverance from the storm and an acknowledgement of his spiritual life with God. Newton passed away in 1807 at the age of 82, the same year that the slave trade was abolished in Britain.

While serving the Church of England as a parish priest, Newton often collaborated with his friend and poet William Cowper in producing hymn texts for his congregation in the small village of Olney. In 1779 their combined efforts produced *Olney Hymns*, a collection of 349 hymns that included the words of Newton's "Amazing Grace." Those words originally appeared under the title "Faith's Review and Expectation."

A few years later in America, Newton's famous words were combined with a plantation melody known as "Loving Lambs." Now called "Amazing Grace," this tune first appeared in 1831 in a shape note hymnal titled *The Virginia Harmony*, compiled by James P. Carrell and David S. Clayton and published in Winchester, Virginia. Since that time, "Amazing Grace" has been performed in a variety of venues as a universal song of hope and peace.

Swing Low, Sweet Chariot

With words rich in biblical imagery, the highly revered spiritual "Swing Low, Sweet Chariot" was in its day a "signal song" or "coded song." It was one of a few spirituals directly related to escaping to the North, for some of the words refer to the activities of the Underground Railroad. Neither a railroad nor underground, such activities consisted of escaped slaves traveling on foot, boat, railcar, wagon or horse, stopping to rest at safe houses in order to find freedom in the North. "Swing Low, Sweet Chariot" was a favorite spiritual of Harriet Tubman (1820–1913), who escaped from slavery in 1849 and who was one of the most famous leaders of the Underground Railroad.

In this spiritual, code words were used to hide the secret meaning of the lyrics. Coded songs allowed the slaves to share their dream of freedom without alarming the slaveholders with threatening words of protest.

For example, "sweet chariot" referred to the Underground Railroad which was going to "swing low" or come down from the North into the slaveholding states. "Comin' for to carry me home" meant that the Underground Railroad was going to take the enslaved Negro to freedom in the North. The words "I looked over Jordan" were a reference to either the Mississippi River or the Ohio River and "a band of angels" was a code for the workers of the Underground Railroad. "Wade in the Water," "Go Down Moses," and "The Gospel Train" are additional coded spirituals which have left us a great cultural heritage.

26. Go, Tell It on the Mountain

SPIRITUAL
Arranged by **PATRICK M. LIEBERGEN**

27. Deep River

SPIRITUAL
Arranged by **PATRICK M. LIEBERGEN**

Deep_____ riv - er, Lord, I

want to cross o - ver in - to camp - ground, I

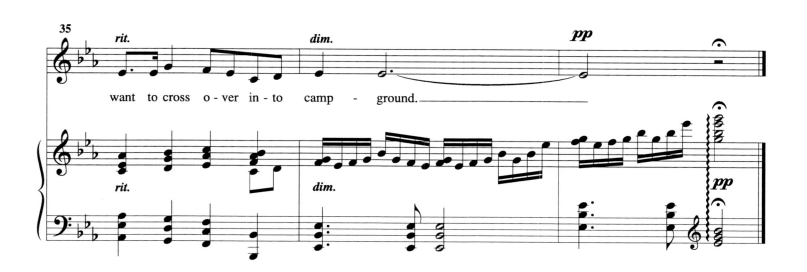

want to cross o - ver in - to camp - ground._____

28. Shenandoah

RIVER CHANTEY
Arranged by **PATRICK M. LIEBERGEN**

way,_____ I'm bound a - way_____ 'cross the wide_____ Mis - sou -
way,_____ I'm bound a - way_____ 'cross the wide_____ Mis - sou -

ri.
ri.

Fare - well my dear,_____ I'm bound to leave you,_____ A -

way_____ you roll - ing riv - er,_____ Oh, Shen - an - doah_____ I'll not de -

29. Amazing Grace

Words by **JOHN NEWTON** (1725–1807)

AMERICAN MELODY
from VIRGINIA HARMONY, 1831
compiled by **JAMES P. CARRELL** *and* **DAVID S. CLAYTON**
Arranged by **PATRICK M. LIEBERGEN**

30. Swing Low, Sweet Chariot

SPIRITUAL
Arranged by **PATRICK M. LIEBERGEN**

Folk Songs from the British Isles

Down by the Salley Gardens

This Irish tune is a unique type of "folk song," for the author of the words is known. They were written by William Butler Yeats, and were first published in 1899 in *Crossways*, a collection of his poems. Yeats was one of the greatest English-speaking poets of the 20th Century and a recipient of the Nobel Prize in Literature in 1923. He is highly revered today as an Irish poet, dramatist and prose writer. Quite active in societies that attempted an Irish literary revival, Yeats promoted Ireland's native heritage throughout his career, writing about its history, folklore and contemporary public life. Yeats often wrote pieces to revive Celtic identity while working against the English rule in Ireland.

This love poem of Yeats is a very simple and heartfelt setting to the melody titled "Down by the Salley Gardens," also known as "The Maids of Mourne Shore." The word "Salley" in this poem refers to a willow tree. Gardens of willows were common in Ireland because the willow rods were used for basket-making and for the thatch roofing of cottages. A "weir" (m. 33) is a fence erected in a stream to catch fish.

Greensleeves
(What Child Is This)

The earliest lyrics of this English folk song were registered to a Richard Jones in 1580, and they were first published in 1584 in *A Handful of Pleasant Delights*. The haunting and beautiful melody was first published in 1652. Few believe the legend that Henry VIII wrote "Greensleeves" during his courtship with Anne Boleyn.

Initially popular mainly in Britain, this tune as been sung to a variety of lyrics over the years. It was the Christmas version by William Chaterton Dix that made it a beloved song throughout much of the world.

Born in Somerset, England in 1837, Dix loved writing poetry and reading classic literature. He became an insurance salesman and settled in Glasgow, Scotland. However, he became suddenly ill at the age of 29 and was eventually confined to a bed in a deep depression. Experiencing a spiritual awakening while praying to God for health, he then produced some of our great hymns, including "Alleluia! Sing to Jesus" and "As with Gladness, Men of Old." Dix wrote the famous words of "What Child Is This" in the Christmas of 1865, calling his work "The Manger Throne." Both the traditional words and Dix's version are presented in this new arrangement.

All Through the Night

This very popular Welsh folk song, originally titled *"Ar Hyd y Nos,"* was first published in *Musical Relicks of the Welsh Bards* by Bard y Brenin in 1784. It has been translated into a number of languages and arranged for a variety of vocal and instrumental ensembles through the centuries. One arrangement was made by Franz Joseph Haydn, who set the original melody and words in 1803 for vocal duet, violin and piano.

The most popular English version of the original Welsh is by Harold Boulton. His words are presented here in this new arrangement. This song is often listed in anthologies as a lullaby, for Boulton's words are meant to be sung to a small child at bedtime.

Early One Morning

The words of this well known English folk song were originally known as either "The Lamenting Maid" or "The Lovesick Maid," and they were included in a number of publications dating back to 1787. However it wasn't until the early nineteenth century that the words were first published with this tuneful and simple melody in William Chapell's collection titled *English National Airs* (1838–1840).

Loch Lomond

This famous Scottish folk song is based on the folk tune "Robin Cushie" ("Kind Robin Loves Me"), which appeared in McGibbon's *Scots Tunes Book I* in 1742. The words are attributed to Lady John Scott (1810-1900) and were first published in *Poets and Poetry of Scotland* in 1876.

"Loch Lomond" is based upon the legend that two of Bonnie Prince Charlie's men (Jacobites) were captured by the English in the Jacobite uprising of 1745. This uprising was an unsuccessful attempt to depose Britain's King George II so that a Scottish King could then rule the United Kingdom (Scotland, England, and Wales). According to the legend, one of the captured men was to be executed at Carlisle and the other one was to be released. The Jacobite to be hanged told the other soldier that in his death, his spirit would take the "low road" and would be in Scotland with his true love near Loch Lomond before his comrade, who would have to return to Scotland by taking the "high road" or miles of high rugged country. Strophic and quite tuneful, this folk song is highly revered by the Scottish people.

31. Down by the Salley Gardens

Words by **WILLIAM BUTLER YEATS** (1865–1939)

IRISH FOLK SONG
Arranged by **PATRICK M. LIEBERGEN**

easy, as the leaves grow on the tree; But

I, being young and foolish with her did not a-
(he)

gree.

In a field by the river my
(his)

32. Greensleeves
(What Child Is This)

Words of "Greensleeves" traditional
Words of "What Child Is This" by
WILLIAM CHATTERTON DIX (1837–1898)

ENGLISH FOLK SONG
Arranged by **PATRICK M. LIEBERGEN**

Green- sleeves, now fare - well and a - dieu, to
So bring Him in - cense, gold and myrrh;— come,

God I pray—— to pros - per thee! For I am still—— thy
one and all,—— to own—— him. The King of kings—— sal -

lov - er true,—— Come once—— a - gain—— and love me.
va - tion bring,—— Let lov - ing hearts—— en - throne Him.

Green - sleeves—— was all my joy,—— Green - sleeves—— was
This, this—— is Christ the King,—— whom shep - herds guard—— and

my de - light, Green - sleeves was my heart of gold,—And
an - gels sing; Haste, haste—— to bring Him laud,—the

who but my La - dy Green - sleeves.
babe,— the son—— of Ma - ry.

33. All Through the Night

Words by **HAROLD BOULTON** (1859–1935)

WELSH FOLK SONG
Arranged by **PATRICK M. LIEBERGEN**

Sleep, my child, and peace at-tend thee All through the night,
While the moon her watch is keep-ing All through the night,

Guard - ian an - gels God will send thee All through the night;
While the wea - ry world is sleep - ing All through the night;

All Through the Night ■ 173

34. Early One Morning

ENGLISH FOLK SONG
Arranged by **PATRICK M. LIEBERGEN**

35. Loch Lomond

SCOTTISH FOLK SONG
Arranged by **PATRICK M. LIEBERGEN**

1. By— yon bon - nie banks and by yon bon - nie braes. Where the
there that we part - ed in yon shad - y glen, On the

sun shines bright on Loch Lo - mond, Where me and my true love will
steep, steep side o' Ben Lo - mond, Where in pur - ple hue the—

ev - er wont to gae On the bon - nie, bon - nie banks o' Loch
High - land hills we view, An' the moon— com - in' out in the

Lo - mond. 3. The wee bird - ies sing and the wild flow - ers spring, And in sun - light the wa - ters are sleep - in', But the bro - ken heart it sees nae sec - ond spring, And the world may not know how we're meet - in'. Oh, ye'll take the high road and

Strongly
sub.
mf

Mexico

Cielito Lindo

Especially popular in California and northern Mexico, *"Cielito lindo"* is a beloved Mexican folk song which is part of the collective musical memory of Latin America. A very popular song for vocalists, it is also performed by choral and instrumental ensembles.

The lilting triple meter of *"Cielito lindo"* is typical of Mexican folk music. In the latter part of the nineteenth century, Mexicans were greatly influenced by the dance forms brought to them by the Europeans, most notably from the court of the Hapsburg Prince Maximilian. These dance forms, such as the waltz and mazurka, were often performed by instrumental ensembles, called mariachi. Today this type of ensemble consists of singer musicians playing trumpets, violins and a variety of guitars.

PRONUNCIATION GUIDE

De la Sie-rra Mo-re-na, cie-li-to lin-do,* vie-nen ba-jan-do,
de la sje-ra   mo-re-na, sje-li-to lin-do,   βje-ne ba-xan-do,

Un par de͜_o-ji-tos ne-gros, cie-li-to lin-do, de con-tra-ban-do.**
un par deo -xi-tos ne-ɣros, sje-li-to lin-do, ðe kon-tɾa-βan-do.

Ay, ay, ay, ay, can-ta͜_y no llo-res,
ai, ai, ai, ai, kan-tai   no jo-ɾes,

Por-que can-tan-do se͜_a le-gran, cie-li-to lin-do, los co-ra-zo-nes.
poɾ-ke   kan-tan-do sea   le-ɣran, sje-li-to lin-do, los ko-ɾa-so-nes.

E-se lu-nar que tie-nes, cie-li-to lin-do, jun-to͜_a la bo-ca,
e-se lu-naɾ ke   tie-nes, sje-li-to lin-do xun-toa   la βo-ca,

No se lo des a na-die, cie-li-to lin-do, que͜_a mi me to-ca.
no se lo ðes a na-ðie, sje-li-to lin-do, kea   mi me to-ka.

Ay, ay, ay, ay…..

Footnote to Spanish Pronunciation

• In multiple syllable words, the syllables that should be stressed are underlined.

• [ɾ] should be flipped.

• [r] should be strongly trilled.

• [β] indicates a voiced "b."

•[ɣ] indicates the voiced form of [x]. The sound of [ɣ] is like the "g" in the English word "go," but with greatly reduced tension and with vibration of the uvula.

• [ð] indicates a voiced "th," as in the English word "then."

TRANSLATION

Down from the Brown Mountains, my sweetheart,*
come descending
A pair of black eyes, my sweetheart, of contraband.**

Ay, ay, ay, ay, sing and don't cry,
Because by singing, my sweetheart, hearts are
made merry.

That mole that you have, my sweetheart, next to
your mouth,
Don't give it to anyone, my sweetheart, because it is mine.

Ay, ay, ay, ay . . .

* *"cielito lindo" is a term of endearment. It translates literally as "beautiful little heaven."*
** *"contrabando" refers to the sweetheart who is "illegal," because she should not be away from the mountains.*

36. Cielito Lindo

MEXICAN FOLK SONG
Arranged by **PATRICK M. LIEBERGEN**

Rhythmically and energetically in one (σ. = ca. 52)

mf

mf

1. De la Sie - rra Mo - re - na, cie - li - to
2. E - se lu - nar que tie - nes, cie - li - to

(mf)

lin - do, vie - nen ba - jan - do,_____ Un par de o -
lin - do, jun - to a la bo - ca,_____ No se lo___

- ji - tos ne - gros, cie - li - to lin - do, de___ con - tra -
___ des a na - die, cie - li - to lin - do, que a___ mi me

Israel

Hatikvah

Hatikvah means "the hope." This song is an uplifting message of hope for the Jewish people, that they may someday return to the land of their forefathers as prophesied in the Hebrew Bible. The Jewish people were exiled from Israel when the temple in Jerusalem was destroyed. During the two thousand years of exile, the Jewish people prayed for their return to Israel while facing in the direction of Jerusalem. The word "Zion" in this song is synonymous with Israel and Jerusalem.

The words of *"Hatikvah"* were written by the Galician poet Naphtali Herz Imber, an English poet originally from Bohemia who moved to Palestine in 1882 to write essays, poetry and articles for Hebrew periodicals. Imber's poem was written in 1878 and was published in 1886 in Imber's journal *Barkai*.

The Moldavian born Samuel Cohen became familiar with Imber's poem when Imber went to Rishon L'Zion in 1882 where Cohen was living. Originally titled *"Tikvatenu,"* Imber's poem was set by Cohen to a Moldavian-Rumanian folk song called *"Carul cu Boi"* ("Cart and Ox"). This folk song melody was well-known in the later part of the nineteenth century; Bedrich Smetana also used it when he wrote his symphonic poem *The Moldau* in 1874.

Highly revered as a Zionist anthem, *"Hatikvah"* has been sung at Zionist Congresses. In 1948 it became the official national anthem of Israel. This song represents the prayers of the Jewish people, and it also symbolizes a free homeland full of peace and harmony.

Provided here is a transliteration of the Hebrew found in many sources, with the IPA guide below the text.

PRONUNCIATION GUIDE

Kol od ba-le-vav   p'ni-mah
kɔl ɔd bɑ-l[ɛe]-vɑv pəni-mɑ

Ne-fesh Ye-hu-di   ho-mi-yah,
nɛ-fɛsh jə-h[ʊu]-d[ɹi] hɔ-m[ɹi]-jɑ,

Ul-fa-a-tey   miz-rach ka-di-mah
ulə-fɑ-ɑ-t[ɛe] miz-rɑx kɑ-d[ɹi]-mɑ

A-yin le-tzi-on   tzo-fi-yah.
ɑ-j[ɹi]n lə-ts[ɹi]-ɔn tsɔ-f[ɹi]-jɑ.

Od lo av-dah tik-va-te-nu,
ɔd lɔ ɑv-dɑ t[ɹi]k-vɑ-t[ɛe]-nu,

Ha-tik-vah bat shnot al-pa-yim,
hɑ-t[ɹi]k-vɑ bɑt ʃənɔt ɑl-pɑ-j[ɹi]m,

Li-hyot am chof-shi be-ar-tze-nu,
l[ɹi]-hjɔt ɑm xɔf - ʃi bə-ɑɾ-ts[ɛe]-n[ʊu],

E-retz   Tzi-on   vi-ru-sha-la-yim.
[ɛe]-ɾ[ɛe]ts ts[ɹi]-jɔn v[ɹi]-ɾ[ʊu]-ʃɑ-lɑ-j[ɹi]m.

Footnotes to Hebrew Pronunciation

• In multiple syllable words, the syllables which should be stressed are underlined, as dictated by the natural musical pulsations of this westernized musical setting.

• [ɾ] should be flipped.

• [r] should be trilled.

• The following vowels should be pronounced as indicated:
The "u" in the transliteration should be pronounced as either [u] or [ʊu], which is a combination of [ʊ] and [u].

The "i" in the transliteration should be pronounced as [ɹi] which is a combination of [ɹ] and [i].

The "e" in the transliteration should be pronounced either as [ə] or as [ɛe]. [ɛe] is a combination of [ɛ] and [e].

TRANSLATION

As long as deep in the heart,
The soul of a Jew yearns,
And towards the East,
An eye looks to Zion.
Our hope is not yet lost,
The hope of two thousand years,
To be a free nation in our land,
The land of Zion and Jerusalem.

37. Hatikvah
(The Hope)

Words by **NAFTALI HERZ IMBER** (1856–1909)

Setting of "*Carul cu Boi*" by
SAMUEL COHEN (1870–1940)
Arranged by **PATRICK M. LIEBERGEN**

3. Ave Maria

FLUTE (or C-Instrument)

GIULIO CACCINI (1546–1618)
Arranged by **PATRICK M. LIEBERGEN**

13. O Come, O Come, Emmanuel
(Veni, veni, Emanuel)

FLUTE (or C-Instrument)

15th c. French melody
Adapted by **THOMAS HELMORE** (1811–1890)
Edited and arranged by **PATRICK M. LIEBERGEN**

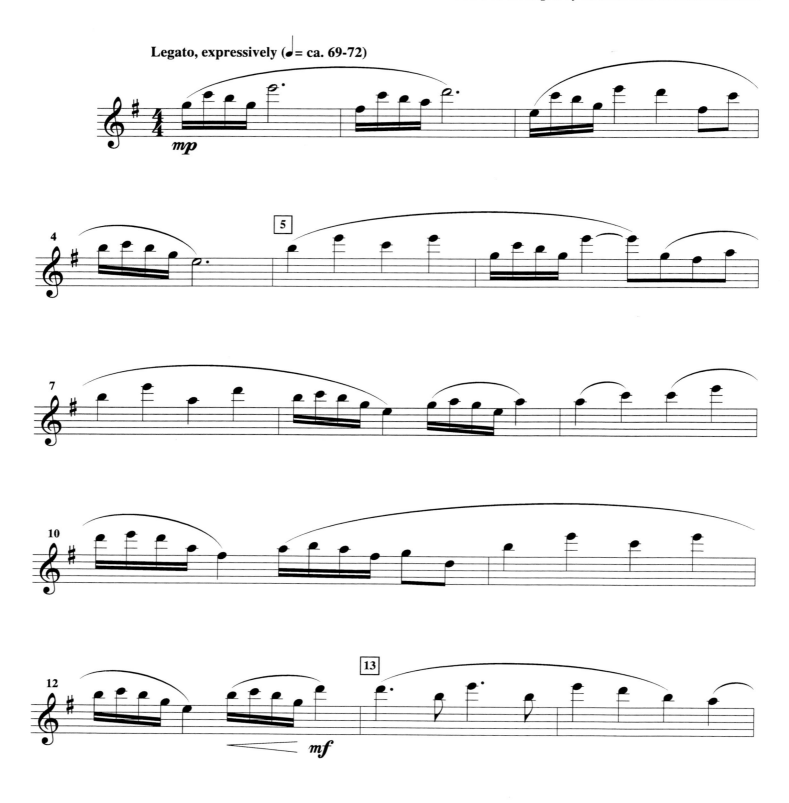

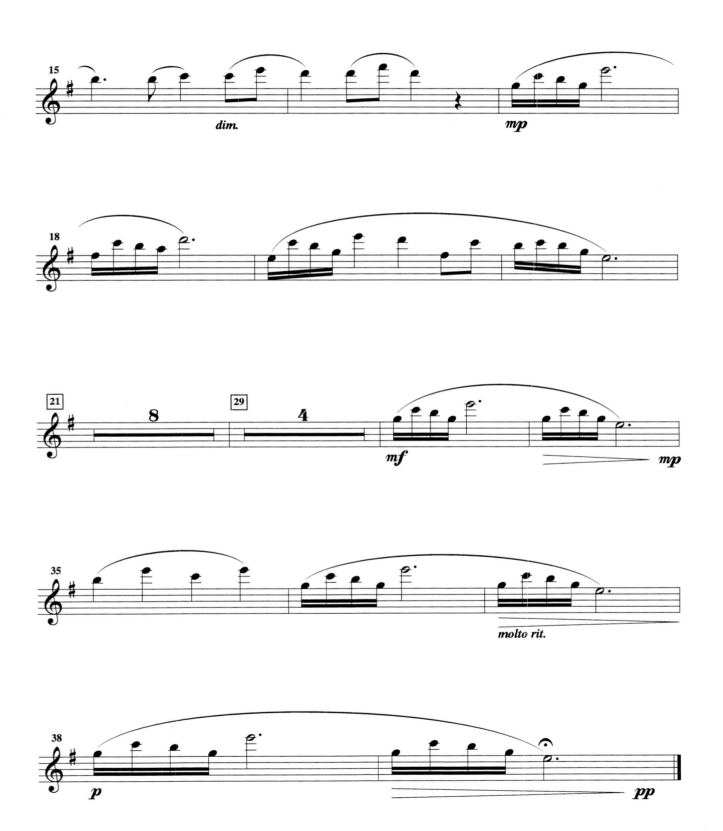

15. Panis angelicus
(O Lord, I Pray to Thee)

FLUTE (or C-Instrument)

from *Messe à 3 voix*
by **CÉSAR FRANCK** (1822–1890)
Edited and arranged by **PATRICK M. LIEBERGEN**

15. Panis angelicus
(O Lord, I Pray to Thee)

from *Messe à 3 voix*
by **CÉSAR FRANCK** (1822–1890)
Edited and arranged by **PATRICK M. LIEBERGEN**

CELLO

International Phonetic Alphabet
Pronunciation Guide

IPA symbols used in this book with equivalent sounds in English:

Vowels

[a]	(first part of) light [laɪt], shout [ʃaʊt]
[ɑ]	d<u>a</u>rk, b<u>a</u>lm, f<u>a</u>ther
[e]	c<u>a</u>me, m<u>a</u>ke, g<u>a</u>ve
[ɛ]	l<u>e</u>t, m<u>a</u>ny, fr<u>ie</u>nd
[ə]	lem<u>o</u>n, ev<u>e</u>n, ov<u>e</u>n
[i]	s<u>ee</u>, mach<u>i</u>ne, rec<u>ei</u>ve
[ɪ]	s<u>i</u>t, b<u>u</u>sy, g<u>y</u>m
[o]	<u>o</u>bey, b<u>o</u>de, cl<u>oa</u>k
[ɔ]	sh<u>o</u>re, c<u>ou</u>ght, r<u>aw</u>
[ʊ]	b<u>oo</u>k, l<u>oo</u>k, g<u>oo</u>d
[u]	y<u>ou</u>, wh<u>o</u>, t<u>oo</u>th

Semivowels

[j]	<u>y</u>es, on<u>i</u>on, <u>y</u>ou
[w]	<u>w</u>as, s<u>w</u>eet, s<u>u</u>ede

Dipthongs:

[ɑɪ]	cr<u>y</u>, n<u>i</u>ght, p<u>ie</u>
[ɑʊ]	ab<u>ou</u>t, h<u>ou</u>se. n<u>ow</u>
[ɔʏ]	Used in German, this indicates a similar sound to the English dipthong [ɔɪ], as in t<u>oy</u>, ch<u>oi</u>ce, j<u>oy</u>. However, in German, the second part of the dipthong [ʏ] is rounder than the corresponding second part in English.

Consonants

[b]	<u>b</u>aby, <u>b</u>at, <u>bubb</u>le
[d]	<u>d</u>og, be<u>d</u>, <u>d</u>o
[f]	li<u>f</u>e, <u>f</u>ire, i<u>f</u>
[g]	<u>g</u>o, ci<u>g</u>ar, twi<u>g</u>
[dʒ]	<u>j</u>oy, <u>j</u>et, <u>g</u>enerous
[h]	<u>h</u>ouse, <u>wh</u>o, <u>h</u>it
[k]	<u>c</u>at, tac<u>k</u>le, <u>ch</u>oir
[ks]	a<u>x</u>, e<u>x</u>treme, he<u>x</u>agon
[l]	a<u>l</u>to, a<u>ll</u>e<u>l</u>uia, <u>l</u>et
[m]	hy<u>mn</u>, <u>m</u>other, hu<u>m</u>
[n]	pa<u>n</u>, s<u>n</u>ail, <u>n</u>ose
[ŋ]	si<u>ng</u>, ha<u>ng</u>, goi<u>ng</u>
[p]	<u>p</u>ut, su<u>pp</u>er, sa<u>p</u>
[s]	<u>s</u>tep, <u>s</u>pin, cour<u>s</u>e
[ʃ]	<u>sh</u>oot, pu<u>sh</u>, <u>sh</u>ine
[t]	hi<u>t</u>, ba<u>tt</u>le, <u>t</u>ube
[tʃ]	<u>c</u>ello, hi<u>tch</u>, <u>ch</u>eer
[ð]	ra<u>th</u>er, <u>th</u>en, <u>th</u>ose
[v]	<u>v</u>ery, ner<u>v</u>e, <u>v</u>isit
[z]	no<u>s</u>e, <u>z</u>ebra, <u>z</u>oo
[ʒ]	lei<u>s</u>ure, vi<u>s</u>ion, A<u>s</u>ia

Additional IPA Symbols Used In This Book:

[ː]   Indicates to lengthen the previous vowel or consonant.

Vowels

[ø]   tongue position for [e] and lip position for [o], as in the French word "peux"— [pø], and in the German word "schönen"— [ʃø-nən].

[œ]   tongue position for [ɛ] and lip position for [ɔ], as in the French word "Sauveur"— [so-<u>vœɾ</u>], and in the German word "Köpfchen"— [<u>kœpf</u>-çən].

[y]   tongue position for [i] and lip position for [u], as in the French word "plus"— [ply], and in the German word "glüht"— [glyt].

[ʏ]   tongue position for [ɪ] and lip position for [ʊ], as in the German word "drückten"— [<u>drʏk</u>-tən].

[ɥ]   Indicates to glide the [y] vowel, by quickly moving from the slightly sustained [y] sound to the next sound, as in the French word "nuit"— [nɥi].

[˜]   Indicates that the vowel below it should be nasalized, as in the French word "mon"— [mɔ̃].

Consonants

[β]   Indicates a voiced "b", as in the Spanish word "contrabando"— [kon-tra-<u>βan</u>-do].

[ç]   Indicates that the tongue should be placed close to the palate in the position for the vowel [i] while at the same time sharply blowing air through that opening. Known as the "ich" sound, it closely resembles the initial aspirate sound in the English word "<u>h</u>ue" that is emphasized.

[ɲ]   Indicates that the tip of the tongue should be in contact with the lower front teeth while the front of the tongue is raised and pressed against the front of the hard palate. Nasality is then produced when breath passes through the nose, as in the Italian word "ogni"— [oɲɪ]

[x]   Indicates that an aspirant, voiceless sound should be produced by blowing air to cause friction between the soft palate and the back of the tongue, which is moved up toward the soft palate, as in the German word "Ach"— [ax].

[ɣ]   Indicates the voiced form of [x]. The sound of [ɣ] is like the "g" in the English word "go", but with greatly reduced tension and with vibration of the uvula, as in the Spanish word "negros"— [<u>ne</u>-ɣros].

[ɾ]   a singular, flipped "r"

[r]   a trilled "r"

[ʎ]   indicates a similar sound to [lj] in the word "million"— [<u>mɪ</u>-ljən], requiring only one tongue action, as in the Italian word "giglio"— [<u>dʒi</u>-ʎɔ].

Sources

Bach, Johann Sebastian. "Jesu Joy of Man's Desiring." *Herz und Mund und Tat und Leben. Johann Sebastian Bachs Werke*. Ed. Bach-Gesellschaft. Vol. 30. Leipzig, Breitkopf & Härtel, 1926. 47 vols.

Bishop, Henry R. "Love Has Eyes." *The Farmers Wife*. London: Goulding, D'Almaine, Potter & Co., 18--.

Brahms, Johannes. "Wiegenlied." *Johannes Brahms Sämtliche Werke*. Ed. H. Gál and E. Mandyczewski. Vol. 24. Leipzig: Breitkopf & Härtel, 1927. 26 vols.

Copland, Aaron. "At The River." *Old American Songs, Set II*. New York: Boosey & Hawkes, 1954.

Dowland, John. "Come Again, Sweet Love Doth Now Invite." *The First Booke of Songes or Ayres*. London: Peter Short, 1597.

Handel, George Frideric. "Where'er You Walk." *Semele. George Friedrich Händels Werke*. Ed. Friedrich Chrysander. Vol. 7. Leipzig: Brietkopf & Härtel, 1860. 96 vols.

Head, Michael. "When I Think Upon The Maidens." New York: Boosey & Hawkes, 1920.

Lully, Jean Baptiste "Bois épais." *Amadis. Oeuvres complètes de J.-B. Lully*. Vol. 10. Published under the direction of Philippe Quinault. Paris: Éditions Lully, 1939. 10 vols.

Mendelssohn, Felix. "O Rest In The Lord." *Elijah. Werke*. Ser. 13. Leipzig: Breitkopf & Härtel, 1877. 19 ser.

Monro, George. "My Lovely Ceclia." Arr. H. Lone Wilson. New York: Boosey & Hawkes, 1926.

Parisotti, Alessandro. "Se tu m'ami." *Arie Antiche*. Vol. 1. Milan: Ricordi, 1885. 3 vols.

Peri, Jacopo. "Gioite al canto mio." *Euridice*. Florence: Giorgio Marescotti, 1600.

Purcell, Henry. "I Attempt From Love's Sickness." *The Indian Queen*. Ed. E. J. Dent. Vol. 19. London: The Purcell Society, 1912. 32 vols.

Quilter, Roger. "Sigh No More, Ladies." *Four Shakespeare Songs*. Third Set. New York: Boosey & Hawkes, 1933.

Schubert, Franz. "Heidenröslein." *Franz Schuberts Werke*. Eds. Johannes Brahms, Ignaz Brüll, Anton Door, Jul. Epstein, J. N. Fuchs, J. Ganbacher, J. Hellmesberger, Eusebius Mandyczewski. Ser. 20, Vol. 3, No. 114. Leipzig: Breitkopf & Härtel, 1897. 21 ser.

Schumann, Robert. "Die Lotosblume." *Robert Schumann's Werke*. Ed. Clara Schumann. Ser. 13, Vol. 1, No. 2. Leipzig: Breitkopf & Härtel, 1882. 14 ser.

Stölzel, Gottfried Heinrich. "Bist du bei mir." *Notenbuch der Anna Magdalena Bach. Johann Sebastian Bachs Werke*. Ed. Bach-Gessellschaft. Vol. 39. Leipzig: Breitkopf & Härtel, 1926. 47vols.

Vaughan Williams, Ralph. "The Call" *Five Mystical Songs*. London: Stainer & Bell, 1911.

Alphabetical Index of Titles